North York Moors

Dalesman Publishing Company
Stable Courtyard, Broughton Hall,
Skipton, North Yorkshire BD23 3AE

First Edition 1998

Text © Nick Channer 1998
Maps by Jeremy Ashcroft
Cover photograph: Farndale by Roger Kilvington

A British Library Cataloguing in Publication
record is available for this book

ISBN 185568 125 0

Printed by Midas Printing (HK) Ltd

North York Moors

Nick Channer

Series editor Terry Marsh

DALESMAN

North York Moors

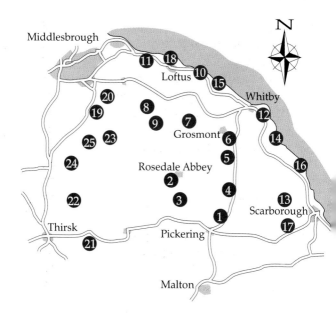

Contents

Alec Wright

Farming on the North York Moors

INTRODUCTION

East of the Pennines and north of the Yorkshire Wolds, the North York Moors National Park is a walker's paradise, offering numerous opportunities to escape the pressures of the modern world and savour the region's unique sense of space and distance. Despite its annual influx of twelve million visitors, the National Park often exudes an air of overwhelming solitude and isolation, as though its more remote tracts of moorland and forest have been completely cut off from the rest of civilisation.

This is where those on foot can sometimes walk for miles without meeting another living soul. Even the designated North Yorkshire and Cleveland Heritage Coast, defining the National Park's eastern boundary, and a perfect natural playground for those who enjoy invigorating tramps over breezy clifftops and open headlands, can, in places, seem surprisingly bereft of people.

Many visitors tour the region by car, which can create problems for the local environment, but the only real way to capture the true spirit and essence of the moors and coast is to go out and explore them on foot, stimulating a wonderful sense of freedom and creating an empathy with the landscape. Walking through the seasons is always a rewarding experience, and the North York Moors National Park is no exception. In autumn, the bursts of deciduous woodland and swathes of invasive bracken conspire to create a dazzling spectrum of colours, and even in the depths of winter, a hike on the hills or a stroll by the sea often reveals something new and unexpected.

Covering 554 miles (1,436km) and acknowledged as an internationally important site for upland breeding birds, the North York Moors National Park is characterised by the rich diversity of its landscape. A vast, intricately-woven tapestry of heather moorland, narrow valleys, rolling dales, broad-leaved woodland and extensive conifer forests, few places in Britain offer such variety and breadth of terrain.

Cut by wooded 'wykes' and bays and once the haunt of smugglers, the North Yorkshire and Cleveland Heritage Coast, extending for 36 miles (58km) between Saltburn-by-the-Sea and Scalby Ness, is distinguished by its soaring cliffs and chain of picturesque fishing villages. The popular holiday resorts of Whitby and Scarborough are the two largest settlements on this stretch of coastline, rich in fossils and minerals and protected for its outstanding natural beauty and historic interest.

The region's origins are rooted firmly in the Jurassic period, its strata characterised by a rich mixture of oolitic limestone, Lias shale and kimmeridge clay. The Great Ice Age later shaped and sculpted the landscape before man first made his mark here during the Middle Stone Age, some 8,000 years ago. The Romans took an interest in the North York Moors but did not exploit their potential in the way they did other parts of Britain, though the Heritage Coast is littered with the remains of their defensive signal stations. The Danes, too, developed a liking for the area, populating the Hambleton Hills and the fertile country of the Cleveland range.

But it was during the 11th century, under William the Conqueror, that the North York Moors witnessed their bleakest period. Soon after William was crowned, the English saw fit to rebel against their new king; William quelled the rising, but in so doing destroyed vast tracts of land, burned down houses and slaughtered many people. As a precaution against further insurrection, and as a symbolic endorsement of his great power and influence, the king built many fortresses and castles in the region.

The North York Moors National Park's immense popularity with visitors owes much to its timeless beauty and majestic scenery. But long before it became a favourite holiday destination, the region's economy was supported by alum, jet and ironstone mining, and the legacy of deep scars, shale tips and spoil heaps is a permanent reminder of the key role this area played during those years of industrial activity. Today, more than eighty per cent of the North York Moors, designated a National Park in 1952, is privately owned and, as well as being a natural focus for outdoor recreational activities, the region is an important working environment sustained by agricultural estates, commercial forestry and quarrying.

Apart from one linear route, all the walks in this guide are circular and have been chosen to reflect the rare beauty and magic of the moors and coast, illustrating the region's highly individual character and identity. To make it easier, the book divides the routes into three logical sections, each demonstrating the various characteristics and traits found within the National Park and Heritage Coast. The described walks take advantage of the region's 1,200-mile/1,920km network of public footpaths and bridleways. Some of the routes follow permitted paths and tracks; permission has been granted for them to be used by readers of this guide. Many of the walks also make good use of a variety of old transport routes, including dismantled railways and drovers' roads.

Access by Road

The North York Moors National Park is well served by a good network of routes. The A1 and A19 skirt the moors to the west, providing easy access from the M62 and M18 to the south, and the A66 crosses the Pennines to meet the M6 at Penrith. The A170 runs along the National Park's southern boundary, between Thirsk and Scarborough, and is a busy holiday route during the summer. Two popular routes, the A169 and A171, cross the eastern moors, connecting Pickering and Scarborough with Whitby, Guisborough and Middlesbrough. The A174 runs along the coast between Whitby and Middlesbrough.

Public Transport

Rail: By train, the North York Moors and Heritage Coast can be reached from many parts of the country. There are mainline stations at Northallerton, Thirsk, Middlesbrough and Scarborough. The Esk Valley Railway serves communities between Middlesbrough and Whitby. The North York Moors Railway operates services between Pickering and Grosmont, with connecting trains for Whitby, Middlesbrough and the Esk Valley.

Bus: The National Park is served by a good network of coach and minibus services, linking many of the region's most popular attractions. The Moorsbus operates on Sundays and Bank holidays between early May and late September, and on Tuesdays and Wednesdays during August. Acknowledged as an environmentally friendly way of exploring the region, the Moorsbus provides more than 200 services on the days it operates and an all-day ticket enables passengers to use the bus service as many times as they wish. Look for the yellow triangular symbol on all Moorsbuses.

Accommodation

The North York Moors National Park has a wide selection of country pubs, guest houses, hotels, self-catering accommodation, campsites and youth hostels. There is a greater concentration of holiday accommodation on the Heritage Coast – particularly at Whitby and Scarborough. Youth hostels in the region are at Osmotherley, Helmsley, Wheeldale, Lockton, Scarborough, Boggle Hole and Whitby.

Equipment

Always be prepared when walking in the great outdoors – that is the cardinal rule. A stout pair of walking shoes or boots is essential and extra layers of clothing are recommended in wintry conditions. Take the necessary precautions on the more elevated routes and carry emergency rations, as well as a compass for the moorland expanses – just in case. Whatever the season, whatever the length of the walk, always carry waterproof clothing. Some exposed stretches of the North York Moors and Heritage Coast can be cool and breezy, even at the height of summer.

June and March are the driest months, while June, July, August and September are the warmest. The months with the highest rainfall are November, January and August.

Maps

The North York Moors National Park is covered by a series of Ordnance Survey maps. For the walks contained in this book, you will need one or more of the following:

Outdoor Leisure Maps

Sheet 26: North York Moors: Western area

Sheet 27: North York Moors: Eastern area

Landranger Sheets

93: Middlesbrough & Darlington

94: Whitby

99: Northallerton & Ripon

100: Malton & Pickering

101: Scarborough & Bridlington

Long Distance Walks

The three most famous long-distance routes to cross the region are the Cleveland Way, Coast to Coast Walk and the Lyke Wake Walk. However, the National Park also has many other lesser-known routes, including the Esk Valley Walk, the Esk Dale Way, the Derwent Way and the White Rose Walk.

The Cleveland Way

Officially opened in 1969, the horseshoe-shaped Cleveland Way is Britain's second oldest long-distance path. Keeping close to the North York Moors National Park's boundary for much of the way, the 93-mile (150km) route divides into two distinct halves. Beginning at Helmsley, the path follows the escarpment of the Hambleton and Cleveland Hills before heading across country to Saltburn. From here it follows the Heritage Coast south to Filey Brigg.

Coast to Coast Walk

One of Britain's most spectacular long-distance

treks, the 190-mile (305km) Coast to Coast Walk was pioneered by the late Alfred Wainwright, doyen of the walking fraternity and a highly-respected author and authority on the upland regions of northern England and Scotland. The walk cuts across the Lake District, Yorkshire Dales and North York Moors, spanning the width of England between St Bees on the Cumbrian west coast and Robin Hood's Bay on the North Yorkshire and Cleveland Heritage Coast.

Lyke Wake Walk

A 40-mile (64km) challenge walk which must be completed within 24 hours to qualify for membership of the Lyke Wake Club. Devised in 1955 by the late Bill Cowley, a local farmer, the route, now badly eroded in places, begins at Scarth Wood Moor, the most westerly point of the Cleveland range, and finishes at Ravenscar on the Heritage Coast. Much of the Lyke Wake Walk is across open heather moorland, following old 'corpse roads', originally used to carry the dead to their final resting place.

Remember

PROTECT plants, trees and wildlife

GUARD against all risk of fire – forest and moorland are particularly susceptible

KEEP dogs and domestic animals under control

LEAVE dogs at home at lambing and nesting times

STAY AWAY from the active grouse moors between 12 August and 10 December

OBSERVE all signs – do not leave open or obstruct gates

OBSERVE – not inspect – old mine and quarry workings

AVOID damaging walls, fences, hedges, signs and buildings

RESPECT others' property and the work of the countryside

CONTRIBUTE to the peace and quiet of the North York Moors and Heritage Coast.

THE CENTRAL MOORS AND DALES

This part of the North York Moors includes some of the finest scenery in the National Park – a haven for walkers and naturalists. Between the endless, rolling expanses of open moorland lie glorious green dales characterised by their pretty villages, sylvan glades, peaceful pastures and tree-shaded becks.

Rosedale, with its fascinating industrial heritage, attracts large numbers of visitors, while Esk Dale carves a glorious passage between rolling hills and swathes of moorland, carrying its tranquil salmon river east towards the North Sea. Several routes in this section follow stretches of the Esk Valley Walk, a 30-mile (48km) trail linking the source of the Esk in Westerdale with its mouth at Whitby.

But it is the openness of the lofty moors that draws the true walker, captivating those who genuinely appreciate the splendours of majestic scenery, where the views seem to stretch to infinity and the purple tint of heather smudges distant, uncluttered landscapes. It was James Herriot who considered that the soul of the North York Moors lay in the remote rural heartland of the Central Moors and Dales and he was probably right. Here, the landscape weaves its own distinctive spell of magic.

However, no visit to the North York Moors is complete without taking a nostalgic steam train ride into the past, rekindling fond memories of a time when these great engines were looked upon as the leviathans of railway travel.

Apart from an enforced period of closure during the late 1960s and early 1970s, the North York Moors Railway has carried passengers along one of the most scenic routes in the North of England since the mid-19th century, with miles of afforested gorges, sheltered green valleys and unprotected moorland providing a constant, unfolding backdrop.

Glaisdale, on the Esk Valley Walk

Stanley Bond

1 Pickering to Levisham

This is a linear walk which will appeal to all rail enthusiasts, evoking fond memories of the golden age of steam travel. Beginning at the station in Pickering, the route heads north across open country, with the North York Moors Railway never far from the path, as though acting as its loyal companion. The walk descends through extensive woodland, crossing the railway line at Farwath, before reaching Levisham's ruined church. Its peaceful setting is one of the highlights of this glorious walk. Beyond the village, there are superb views of Levisham station, the route's ultimate destination, and its spectacular wooded setting.

Distance:
8 miles/12.9km
Height gain:
520ft/158m
Walking time:
3¹/₂ hours
Start: Pickering railway station (car park). GR796842.
Finish: Levisham railway station. Check the North York Moors Railway timetable for times of trains to Pickering before setting out.
Type of walk: The walk follows bridlepaths and tracks across agricultural land; steep descents, sometimes slippery.

The market town of Pickering is the headquarters of the North York Moors Railway. It was in May 1836 that one of the wonders of the North of England was officially opened. Like all great ideas, the Whitby to Pickering railway evolved as a dream in the mind of George Stephenson, but by the 1830s the project was reaching fruition. Construction had begun, the dream had turned to reality. The railway's chief role was to help Whitby traders transport their goods inland, but the line also enabled passengers to travel across the moors in safety.

The line eventually closed in the 1960s, after more than 130 years in service. It lay dormant for several years while a group of dedicated enthusiasts campaigned to revive it. Their efforts eventually paid off and in 1973 the line reopened as Britain's second longest preserved railway, running steam-hauled services along 18 miles/29km of track between Pickering and Grosmont.

Leave the station car park by heading towards the road. Bear left immediately before the *stop when lights show* sign and cross the beck, turning right on the opposite bank. Cross a stile and follow the path through a meadow. Avoid the path running up the bank, keeping to the lower route as it passes to the right of some trees on the far side of the meadow. Cross a tarmac lane and follow the path between hedges.

Negotiate another stile, turn right and head for the riverbank. Bear left on reaching the water and follow the path to a gate. Join a track between trees and hedges and at this point steam trains can sometimes be seen on the right, coming in and out of Pickering station. Pass a house and follow the path between banks of undergrowth.

Go through a gate and follow the track between

fields to a galvanised gate. Turn immediately right to join a tarmac path, pass to the right of some houses, go through two white kissing gates either side of the railway track and cross the beck once more. Bear left at the road, pass the signal box at Newbridge and when the road bends left, veer right by a traffic mirror. Follow the *no through road* through the trees to Park Gate, a farmstead. Pass the buildings and about 80yds/m beyond them, veer half left up the bank. The nostalgic sound of trains and an occasional puff of steam are a reminder that the North York Moors Railway is never far from the route of this walk.

Follow the bridleway up through the trees, pass through a gate at the top of the slope and continue on the path as it curves to the left, running alongside a hedge. Some old stone byres can be seen on the left now. Pass through another gate and follow a clear track, with a fence on the right. Drop down to a gate beneath an oak tree and then head diagonally right to join a track by some gorse bushes.

Veer right at the fork, just before West Farm, and follow the track between fields. The character of the countryside is not really typical of the North York Moors on this stretch of the walk, with the accent on arable and dairy farming – a pleasing mixture of open farmland. The route offers few glimpses of the region's renowned heather moorland, though the scenery here is no less attractive.

Follow the track to the right of Blansby Park Farm;

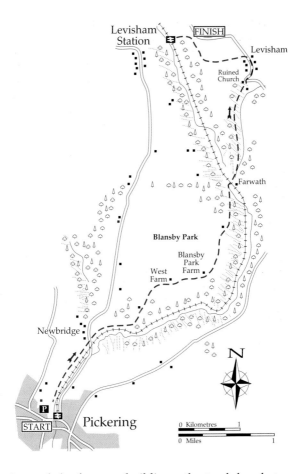

beyond the farm outbuildings, the track bends to the left. Swing right at the fork, avoiding the track on the extreme right, which quickly peters out, and follow the unfenced bridleway to a gate in the far right corner of the field. Continue on the track, with a hedgerow on the right.

At a junction of bridleways, 50yds/m before the remains of some barns at High Blansby, turn right through a gate and head obliquely left across the field towards the woodland. Look for a stile and join a path running between trees and carpets of bracken. Merge with another path and descend steeply towards the railway track. Take great care on this downward stretch as the path can become wet and slippery after rain.

Turn left at the next path junction and the Pickering Beck is visible through the trees, down to the right. After several steps, bear right onto another descending path and head down towards the ford. Turn left to a metal gate, then right to cross a footbridge over the beck. Beyond the bridge lies tiny Farwath – once a remote halt on the North York Moors Railway.

Today, this quiet, inaccessible spot on the railway seems virtually overwhelmed by the huge curtain of woodland rising above it. Apart from walkers and passing steam trains, there is little activity here. Cross the track, pass some old barns and outbuildings and continue ahead. Pass through a gate and follow the bridleway as it curves to the left.

Go through another gate and keep to the track as it cuts through the trees. A galvanised gate marks the woodland boundary and beyond it the track

(Sleights Road) runs across the fields and beside a line of trees. Pass through another gate and continue on the sometimes muddy track. The church tower at Levisham peeps into view at the next gate. Keep going for about 50yds/m, then bear left to join a path under a horse chestnut tree. Follow the path down to a gate followed by a footbridge spanning the Pickering Beck. Take the track past ruined, roofless St Mary's church.

This wonderfully secluded valley church has been a site of worship since the Norman Conquest, though today it is a sadly neglected shadow of its former self. Some sources suggest there was once a village on this site, but the Black Death forced local residents to abandon their homes and establish a community further up the hill.

Despite its isolated setting, the church remained in use until the early 1900s. By the late 1950s, however, St Mary's had fallen into disuse. Without the efforts of the people of Levisham, the church would have been demolished. It is managed today as a controlled ruin. Graves are tended by local families and an open air service is conducted every year. The churchyard contains parts of a Saxon gravestone, bearing a dragon design.

Walk up the steep track and look back for a memorable view of the forlorn church, nestling in the wooded valley. Bear right further up and head for the road. Turn left and follow it round the horseshoe bend, passing the village sign for Levisham. Walk along the broad village street, characterised by its wide, grassy verges and stone cottages.

Turn left just past the church and shortly before the *Horseshoe Inn* and follow the lane between houses and cottages. When the road bends left, cross a stile by a galvanized gate and go straight on along a track running alongside a stone wall. Looking to the left, there are views of the wooded valley and the outward leg of the walk.

Cross the field boundary and continue beside the wall to the next corner. One of the most famous and spectacular views in the North York Moors National Park can be seen at this point. Far below, to the right, the buildings of Levisham station seem to be dwarfed by the wooded gorge, where it carves a passage through Newton Dale. Cross the stile and follow the path down the slope between gorse bushes and then round to the left.

Take care here as the path falls away sharply on one side. A seat is found beyond the next bend, enabling walkers to relax and enjoy the magnificent view of Newton Dale and Levisham station. Descend between gorse and bracken and make for a waymark at the bottom of the slope.

Take the path for the station, crossing the stile just a few yards past the sign. Once in the field, head straight down to a gate in the bottom boundary. Follow the woodland path ahead, which can be slippery at times. Go through a gate, over a beck and out to the road. Turn left and walk down to Levisham station.

2 Rosedale Abbey and North Dale

*This spectacular walk explores two glorious dales –
North Dale and Rosedale. Beginning by a delightfully
placid beck, the path quickly heads for the slopes of North
Dale. The road at the top reveals a breathtaking
panorama of Rosedale, once a centre for ironstone
mining. Extensive plantations shield the path for some
time before the walk heads across pastoral countryside to
finish as it started – by the banks of a beck.*

Distance:	the Milburn Arms
4 miles/6.4km	Hotel. GR725961.
Height gain:	**Type of walk:** *Meadows,*
495ft/151m	*enclosures and fields,*
Walking time:	*then head down through*
2-2¹/₄ hours	*thick woodland*
Start/Finish: *Rosedale*	*plantations to pleasant*
Abbey car park behind	*field paths.*

Today, Rosedale Abbey is an integral part of the North
York Moors tourist trail. However, the scene was very
different during the second half of the 19th century,
when the village played a key role in the Ironstone Age.
It was the dawning of the Industrial Revolution that
signalled a huge demand for ironstone, with much of it
being transported to blast furnaces in the North East for
use in shipbuilding. At the height of this activity, the

population of Rosedale Abbey increased significantly, with more than 5,000 men working in the nearby mines. The crumbling remains of the calcining kilns can be seen outside the village.

From the car park go through the gate and across the sports field to the next gate. Cross a stile and continue towards the next boundary. Keep going with the Northdale Beck running alongside the path, its dark, peaty water in stark contrast to the luxuriant green carpet of the surrounding meadows. Wild garlic grows in the banks and undergrowth on this stretch of the route, its distinctive scent often floating on the breeze. Continue on the path as it skirts the meadows, following the beck through the lower reaches of North Dale. The delightful scene changes little at this early stage of the walk.

Cross numerous field boundaries, following the white waymarks which signify this is a concessionary path, and a little later a bridleway sign and a yellow waymark (public footpath) are seen up ahead. Cross the footbridge spanning the beck and pass through a gate. Avoid a footpath running off to the left and continue ahead on the bridleway as it rises above the beck. Cross a field boundary to reach the road on a bend and join a footpath opposite. There are glorious views of North Dale at this point. Cross the field to a ladder-stile, then head diagonally across the next field to cross its boundary. Keep going along the grassy slopes of the dale, following the vague outline of a path which climbs gradually to a fence.

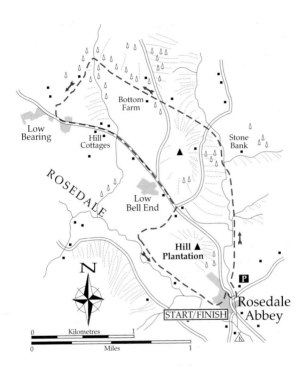

Keep to the left of the boundary, pass some dilapidated farm outbuildings and join a track leading up to a gate by some trees. Turn left and follow the track up the steep slope, pausing at the top to admire the breathtaking views of North Dale. Look for an opening in the bank on the right, leading to a gate beyond which is the road. The view of Rosedale, the walk's next objective, is no less impressive. Turn right for about 40yds/m to a stile on the left. Follow the path down through mixed woodland into the dale. Cross a beck and continue through the trees. On reaching the edge of the woodland, avoid the stile and bear right, following the path along to Clough House. Pass behind it, veer left and make for a stile in the fence.

Turn right and follow the drive to the junction. Bear left and walk down to a gate and seat by the road. Turn left and walk between lines of terraced houses, a reminder of the days when Rosedale Abbey was an important mining community. Some of the houses have unusually long gardens at the front. Cross a beck and at the junction continue ahead towards the centre of Rosedale Abbey. Follow the road round a right-hand bend, then bear right by the buildings of Bell End Farm to join a public footpath, following it down the left boundary of a field. Cross a stile and continue between margins of undergrowth before descending via a flight of stone steps to a footbridge.

Follow the path over several stiles and continue with a field boundary on the right. Pass through a kissing gate and head straight on along the drive leading to a caravan park. Turn left at the public footpath waymark and walk along to the road. Bear right, then left at the junction and keep left at the Abbey Tearoom and Stores, passing the parish church before reaching the junction. Cross the road opposite the *Milburn Arms Hotel* and return to the car park.

3 Lastingham and Spaunton Moor

The delights of Lastingham, an idyllic village sheltering in a sleepy hollow beneath brooding Spaunton Moor, have a habit of distracting walkers before they take their first step on this spectacular journey. The route begins by skirting Spaunton Moor almost as far as Rosedale Abbey, then crosses treeless heather moorland to return to Lastingham. En route, the walk passes the site of an Elizabethan glass furnace before swopping the safe, sheltered environs of the River Seven for the vulnerability of the unprotected moor.

Distance: 7 miles/11.2km	Limited parking in the village.
Height gain: 179ft/55m	**Type of walk:**
Walking time: 3 hours	Enclosures, pastures and Spaunton Moor, where
Start/Finish: Lastingham. GR728904.	the heather is deep and the path not well defined.

Lastingham's ancient crypt church has long been the focus of attention in this charming village. On leaving Lindisfarne in the 7th century, St Cedd chose this site to build a monastery. According to the Venerable Bede, it was "more like the lurking place of robbers and wild beasts than habitations for man". The Danes later desecrated the monastery and the present church of St

Mary dates from the 11th century. The crypt is dedicated to St Cedd and during the 18th century it was, of all things, a venue for cockfighting. One of St Mary's curates used to host a party in the crypt every Sunday evening, while his wife poured pints in the adjacent Blacksmith's Arms.

From the church follow the village street towards Pickering and Rosedale. When the road sweeps to the right, by the sign for Lastingham Grange Hotel, turn left for about 60yds/m and then bear right to join a footpath. Pass a gate and hug the wall to a stile. Follow the path through the trees, cross another stile and continue between enclosures. Veer half left when the path reaches a field and look for a stile in its top boundary. Aim obliquely right to reach another stile and then cross various rectangular enclosures until you reach the edge of Spaunton Moor.

Turn right, following the path alongside the boundary down to the Tranmire Beck. Cross it and head up the bank, aiming slightly left to a gate and stile against the skyline. Continue with the wall on the right until you reach a junction with two tracks. Cross to the second track and follow it to the left. The vast curtain of the 9,390-acre Cropton Forest dominates the view to the right, rising to meet the horizon. The track curves to the right and approaches the buildings of High Askew Farm. Bear left immediately before the gate to pass through a metal gate.

The fencing seen here is part of a programme to restore an area of moorland where the spread of invasive bracken

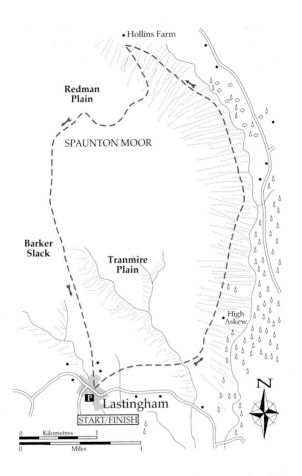

has resulted in the loss of normal heather vegetation. The fences are a temporary measure and will remain until 2001, allowing the heather to regenerate without pressure from grazing animals. The habitat provided by *heather is very important for wildlife conservation, particularly in fragile upland areas.*

Follow the well-worn path between the boundary fence and wall on the right and an area of moorland on the left. When the boundary ends, continue ahead across the moorland. The River Seven, concealed by trees, runs beneath afforested slopes down to the right. In due course, the path hugs a drystone wall on the right, passing a solitary plaque attached to a stone plinth.

The inscription refers to traces of a bygone industry when, in Elizabethan times, skilled craft workers operated a glass furnace here, producing objects of great beauty. Local plants and rocks provided all the right ingredients to make glass and the nearby broad-leaved forests were a valuable source of fuel. Today, the reconstructed furnace is on display in Ryedale Folk Museum in Hutton-le-Hole.

Keep going along the path, sometimes with the boundary wall close by on the right, but always with the tree-fringed Seven and the woodland of Cropton Forest in sight. Two farms loom into view on the opposite bank of the river and soon the buildings of Hollins Farm can be seen up ahead. Turn sharp left about 100 yards/m before the farm and follow the track, sunken in places, up the steep slope. The sweet scent of heather and moorland grass can sometimes be caught on the breeze.

Keep right at the fork and continue on the track, vague and indistinct in places and somewhat obscured by clumps of heather. In places the moorland has been badly burned, leaving little more than blackened areas of stubble on the ground. Cross a path and continue in a south-westerly direction.

On reaching a clear track, turn right and keep right at the next junction. Veer left after a few yards and keep going in a south-westerly direction, following the right of way across a wide expanse of heather moorland until you reach a well-used stony and sandy track. Head south towards Lastingham, the village defined by its sturdy church tower. Pass a seat and a footpath sign for Hartoft on the left. Continue ahead and down the road into Lastingham. Bear right and head back to the church.

4 Skelton Tower and the Bridestones

This outstanding walk captures the essence of the North York Moors, perfectly illustrating the region's rugged beauty and unique character. From the Hole of Horcum, the route makes for Newton Dale's majestic wooded gorge, a breathtaking sight at any time of the year, before climbing to the village of Levisham, where there is a pub. Crossing the A169, the walk makes for the Bridestones, eroded outcrops of rock amid the heather moorland.

Distance:	GR854936.
12 miles/19.5km	*Type of walk: Well-*
Height gain: 250ft/76m	*defined moorland paths*
Walking time: 6 hours	*and tracks, with a stretch*
Start/Finish: Hole of	*of road during the*
Horcum car park.	*middle stage.*

From the car park head north along the verge of the A169 for about 100yds/m. Over to the left is the Hole of Horcum, a huge, grassy bowl that looks as if it might have been scooped out by the hand of a giant. As the road curves left, turn right to join a bridleway for Crosscliff. Follow the metalled track between trees, turning left just before a gate onto a path skirting woodland.

A curious spectacle suddenly looms into view across the

*moors, reminiscent of a blunt pyramid from some angles,
and from others rather like a ruined stronghold from the
distant past. This is RAF Fylingdales and the purpose of
this isolated, oddly-shaped building, replacing three
MOD tracking devices which were famous for years in
this part of Yorkshire for their uncanny resemblance to
golf balls, is to provide Britain with a four-minute
warning in the event of nuclear attack.*

Pass a gate and bridleway on the right and
continue on the path down through trees. Cross a
stile out to the road and make for the footpath to
the side of the *Saltergate Inn*, once the haunt of salt
smugglers. Follow the track over a cattlegrid and
keep to the left of a house, passing to the right of
some corrugated outbuildings. Cross two stiles and
when the fence sweeps away to the left, head for
another stile.

Bear left and follow the path up the gentle slope,
veering a little to the right further on. Cut between
carpets of heather and keep to the worn path along
the foot of the escarpment. Walkers can sometimes
be seen on the top, tiny silhouetted figures just
visible against the skyline. Over to the right lies the
wooded gorge of Newton Dale, through which
steam trains regularly chug on the North York
Moors Railway. This glacial valley evolved more
than 11,000 years ago as a meltwater channel.

The striking remains of Skelton Tower, guarding
Newton Dale, can just be glimpsed in the far
distance, looking minute and vulnerable against
the vastness of the gorge. Continue on the path
towards the landmark. Occasional walkers may

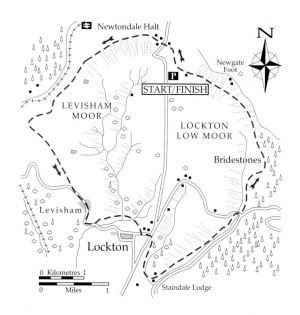

swing into view, but as a rule there are fewer
people on this stretch of the walk than there are
grazing sheep and Highland cattle. Pass a sign on
the right for the Levisham station walk, draw level
with Skelton Tower and continue for a short
distance to a junction of paths.

*Instantly reminiscent of a ruined folly, Skelton Tower
was originally a shooting lodge, built early in the 19th
century for the vicar of Levisham. The tower occupies an
outstanding position, overlooking the thickly afforested
slopes of Newton Dale.*

Turn left here and begin a diagonal climb to the top

of the scarp. Follow the path to the left and head across heather moorland. Continue straight ahead at the corner of a wall. On reaching a gate, join a walled lane leading to a road, then go straight on towards Levisham. Pass the *Horseshoe Inn*, follow the road through the village and on round several bends.

Turn left to follow a right of way above the road. Keep right when the path splits and head east. Pass St Robert's Well and follow the path through trees to Wedland Slack, curving right to reach the road on the east side of Lockton village. Turn left and make for the junction with the A169.

Cross over to the point where two rights of way meet and take the right-hand path through the gate, following it across pastures and enclosures and through several patches of woodland. From Staindale Lodge the route heads north-east, cutting through Holm Woods and running parallel to the Staindale Beck. On reaching the house at Low Staindale, take the stepping stones over the Dove Beck, then bear left to a kissing gate. There is a National Trust sign here for the Bridestones.

Head in a northerly direction between the trees of Dove Dale, making for Needle Point. For almost a mile (1.6km), the path climbs between the steep valleys of Dove Dale and Bridestone.

Thought to be associated with ancient fertility rites, the Bridestones are weathered, curiously sculptured sandstone outcrops which seem to have a slightly surreal quality about them. After a visit to these ancient rocks, the walk heads north-east on a narrow path threading through the heather before skirting the upper part of Dalby Forest, with the boundary fence on the right.

Keep going beside the trees for about 1 mile/1.6km, then follow waymarks across a patch of barren land to join another forest road. Turn left, negotiate a series of stiles, cross another stile at a concrete road and follow the Old Wife's Way back to the car park beside the A169.

5 Goathland and Wade's Causeway

A stone's throw from Goathland, this spectacular walk makes a beeline for one of the region's great natural attractions. Cascading over a towering wall of rock into a leafy gorge, Mallyan Spout is enchanting, drawing many visitors to this corner of the National Park. From here the route makes for the unrelieved expanses of Wheeldale Moor where it joins forces with a section of Wade's Causeway, a well-preserved Roman road. The walk returns to Goathland by passing alongside one of Britain's most isolated youth hostels.

Distance: 7½ miles/12km	**Type of walk:** The path to Mallyan Spout requires careful negotiation. Mainly, the walk follows high-level paths and tracks, finishing with a section of metalled road.
Height gain: 152ft/46m	
Walking time: 3½-4 hours	
Start/Finish: Goathland car park. GR833014.	

Images of Goathland tend to be influenced by its open spaces, broad village greens and deep, wooded ravines. Above all, this remote community conveys a sense of airy spaciousness. Unlike many other villages on the North York Moors, it doesn't take refuge in the shelter of a steep-sided valley; instead it sits out on the moorland.

Many of the houses in Goathland were built after the railway was completed in 1836. Trickling streams and springs trace a course around the village and the stone water troughs seen in Goathland were carved more than 100 years ago to provide much-needed refreshment for thirsty animals. Underfoot, flagstone paths, or trods, line the roads. Dating back to the early 1700s, these routes were used by villagers and packhorses.

From the car park turn right and walk along the main street through the village. Follow the road round the left bend, draw level with the church and turn right immediately before the *Mallyan Spout Hotel* to join a path which descends into the valley via a flight of steps. On reaching the bank of the West Beck, follow the path for Mallyan Spout. Keep the beck on the right, making slow progress along the rock-strewn path. When, at times, it disappears completely, there is no alternative but to scramble along the water's edge. Take care as you negotiate the confusion of rocks and boulders.

The path heads for Mallyan Spout, an impressive 70ft/21m veil of water which spills down over a wall of moss and lichen. Cross and recross the beck before reaching a stile leading out to the road on a bend. Go straight on and when the lane bends left, turn right and follow the bridleway for about 50yds/m. Bear left and take the path across West Beck. Pass a stone cottage and make for a gate with a deer fence. Head out across the rectangular enclosure, look for a gate in the right-hand boundary and follow the path up the slope through trees.

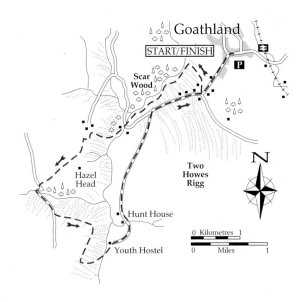

Make for a gate at the top, continue ahead in the field and aim for a gate in the left-hand corner. Head towards a metal gate, bearing right to a gate just before it. Keep to the right of the boundary, make for the field corner and join a moorland lane. Turn left and walk along the lane as far as a grassy path running off to the right, up to a stile. When the path begins to curve right, head straight on alongside the fence. As the fence curves to the left, go straight on through the heather, following the path down to Wheeldale Road.

Turn left and take the road across the Wheeldale Gill. Head up the slope and then look for a footpath on the left, signposted to Wheeldale

Lodge Youth Hostel. The grassy path is indistinct, so aim towards a burst of woodland at the foot of the moorland slopes. Approaching a fence and drystone wall, veer right and join Wade's Causeway. The path's surface is broken and uneven in places, so be careful.

Wade's Causeway, which, according to legend, takes its name from a giant, has the advantage of still being clearly defined on the ground. Built of sandstone slabs and strewn with stones, rocks and the debris of ancient history, the Roman road can be traced across the North York Moors from Malton to Lease Rigg, near Grosmont. Some suggest the road, listed as an ancient monument, once extended as far as the North Yorkshire coast.

Cross a ladder-stile and continue on the ancient road for about 250yds/m. Bear sharp left shortly before the track draws level with afforested slopes and then swing left again on reaching a sculptured rocky outcrop of some size and prominence. Follow the rock-strewn path down through the heather, cross the Wheeldale Beck via stepping stones and pass alongside the youth hostel.

Follow the track past Hunt House, veer right at the fork for Goathland and take the single-track road across the moorland. Pass a footpath on the left and continue to the road junction. Turn right and follow the road, pass Cherry Tree Guest House and keep to the left of Goathland church. Take the road through the village, bearing left for the car park.

6 Grosmont and the Rail Trail

Climbing to the high ground of Sleights Moor, this invigorating walk offers fine views in all directions before descending to the sheltered hamlet of Beck Hole. It is at this point that the character of the walk changes quite significantly, with the route joining the Rail Trail, a popular walkway running beside the delightful, tree-shaded Murk Esk.

Distance:
6¼ miles/10km
Height gain:
580ft/176m
Walking time: 3 hours
Start/Finish: Grosmont.
GR827053. Parking
near the railway station,
or use summertime park
and ride scheme.

Type of walk: The walk
soon heads for tracks
and paths above
Grosmont. Further on,
the route skirts open
moorland before
following a quiet lane
into Beck Hole. The last
leg is on the Rail Trail.

Grosmont, the northern terminus of the North York Moors Railway, dates back to the 19th century, when ironstone was mined in the area. Rows of stone cottages were built to house miners and the village was soon established as a centre of relentless industrial activity – a far cry from the scene today. During the summer Grosmont attracts especially large numbers of sightseers, many of whom visit the village to travel on the much-loved steam trains.

From the car park, walk through Grosmont, cross the railway at the gates and begin a steep climb out of the village. Pass the Station Tavern on the left and follow the road to a junction, veering right for Goathland and Pickering. Keep to the road when it bends right, pass two footpaths on the right and then turn right at the turning for Fair Head Farm.

Follow the track between the farm outbuildings and then strike out between fields to Moor Lane Farm. Pass through a gate on reaching the farm and continue on the track until it reaches a field. Follow the boundary, keeping the wall on the right, and soon a footpath fingerpost can be seen across the enclosure. Turn right, descending into the valley of the Lythe Beck between clumps of coarse grass and bracken. Step over the beck to a gate and then follow the path as it snakes up the slope towards the buildings of Greenlands Farm.

Keep to the left of the farm and pass through a gate. Join a track here and follow it as it winds across open, exposed ground to the road. Cross over and take the path running ahead through the heather. 50yds/m before it merges with another path running in from the left, and 250yds/m before some trees enclosing a house, turn right and follow the grassy path over the moorland. Continue ahead on reaching a track, pass alongside some stone buildings and bear left to a house.

Keep the wall on the left and follow the narrow

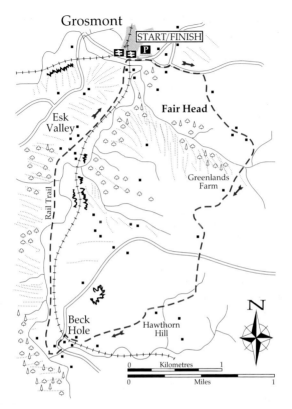

path, which can become overgrown with bracken. On reaching the wall corner, veer half right and follow the path through the bracken and scrub. Bear sharp left at one point and make for a track. Turn right, walk along to a footpath sign and take the lane to the left of the farm. Bear sharp left at the next junction, cross the railway and follow the road down into the hamlet of Beck Hole.

Pass the *Birch Hall Inn*, a delightful pub-cum-village shop, and bear immediately right, following the path to the route of the Rail Trail. Turn right, cross the Eller Beck and head towards Grosmont.

The 3 mile/4.8km Rail Trail runs between Grosmont and Goathland, following the trackbed of the long-abandoned Pickering to Whitby railway. Opened in 1836 and built by George Stephenson as a horse-drawn tramway, the line, which was later used by steam locomotives, remained in commission until 1865 when it was superseded by what is now the North York Moors Railway. However, the old line made something of a comeback in the early part of the 20th century when it was used to serve an autocar service between Whitby and Beck Hole during the summer.

Follow the signs for Grosmont and the Rail Trail, the path crossing and running beside the scurrying Murk Esk. Pass a solitary house and soon the trail reaches the hamlet of Esk Valley, consisting of a seemingly endless terrace of cottages and a former chapel. A peaceful spot now, this was once a community inhabited by workers employed at the nearby ironstone mines. Several buildings here were used as workshops and mine offices.

Beyond Esk Valley, the path runs immediately adjacent to the line of the North York Moors Railway, passing several sheds and sidings, with old rolling stock and various locomotives in different states of repair and restoration. Follow the Rail Trail along the edge of woodland and soon the buildings of Grosmont and its station can be seen down below. Turn right at this point and follow the path down through trees to a gate. Bear left just beyond it and take the Rail Trail down beside St Matthew's church.

Turn sharp left a few yards from the railway track and head for what is understood to be the world's earliest passenger railway tunnel. Built by George Stephenson between 1833-35, as part of the Whitby to Pickering railway, the first carriages were horse-drawn and carried a maximum of ten passengers. The tunnel, which today is used only by pedestrians and is very well lit, leads to the Grosmont Locomotive Depot. Return to the Rail Trail, cross a footbridge and walk back to the centre of Grosmont.

An engine in steam at Grosmont station

John A Ives

7 Lealholm

Views of the Esk valley provide a constant backdrop on this glorious walk which begins with a gentle climb to the fertile, rolling country immediately south of Lealholm. Returning to the valley bottom, the route coincides with a delightful stretch of the Esk Valley Walk, keeping close to the river as it snakes through the lush countryside.

Distance:
4¼ miles/7km
Height gain: 214ft/65m
Walking time: 2 hours
Start/Finish: Lealholm.
GR764076.
Type of walk: After a spell on the road, the walk traces a route across the slopes of the Esk valley, following field paths, tracks and minor lanes. The last lap is alongside the river, over firm paths and tracks.

With its arched bridge, charming cottages, stepping stones and grassy banks, Lealholm is acknowledged as one of the prettiest villages in the Esk valley. Originally an Anglican settlement – the name means 'among the twigs' – Lealholm was a favourite haunt of Canon Atkinson, vicar of nearby Danby, who wrote in his book Forty Years in a Moorland Parish: "Elsewhere you must go in search of beautiful views; here they offer themselves to be looked at."

From the car park turn left towards Glaisdale and cross the River Esk. Pass the *Board Inn* and continue

48

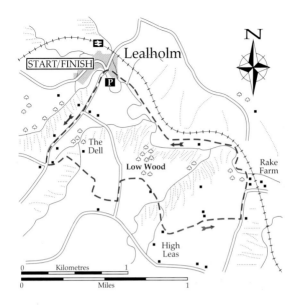

along the road, out of the village. Avoid a turning on the left for Glaisdale, pass a track and cattlegrid and keep going to Mill Lane Farm. Bear left and cut between the outbuildings to a gate. Walk down the field, making for a stile about 50yds/m to the left of a gate in the bottom, tree-lined boundary.

Cross the next field, heading for a wooden gate in the drystone wall. Cross a footbridge spanning a beck and then go straight up the steep slope to a stile in the top right-hand corner of the field. Keep the wall on the right in the next field and make for a stile in the corner. Turn right here and follow two sides of a field until a stile is reached, leading out to the road.

Bear left and follow the road, with a splendid view across Esk Dale. Take the next signposted footpath on the right and follow the track all the way to the farm. Pass through three gates, keeping to the left of the house, and head down the slope to a stile in the bottom corner, by a line of trees. Continue ahead in the next field, keeping the tree-shaded beck close by on the right.

Head for the stables and outbuildings of a farm and turn left at the junction of tracks. Cross a second drive after about 50yds/m and take the rough track through the bracken. Pass through a gate and follow the track to a house. Take the paved path to the right of it and bear right onto the drive, following it to the road. Bear left and descend into the valley. When the lane bends right by Rake Cottage, go straight on down the track, following a stretch of the Esk Valley Walk.

Cross the Esk at the footbridge and bear immediately left. As the track approaches the railway bridge, veer left to join a path running through the bracken. This stretch of the walk includes several surprises. The sturdy stone structure of the railway bridge suddenly looms large on the right, whilst the Esk can be seen scurrying through the trees far below, enhancing Esk Dale's charming, unspoilt setting.

Skirt a field, which echoes to the restful lilt of the adjacent river, and approach the buildings of Underpark Farm. Pass through the metal gate to the left of them and follow the track to a sign for the Esk Valley Walk. Take the track in a westerly direction; the Esk runs close to the route of the walk, meandering delightfully through the dale. Cross a cattlegrid and pass some cottages just before the car park at Lealholm.

Lealholm

8 Danby

The scenery on this walk is a sheer delight. With its swathes of rolling moorland and lush, bracken-covered hillslopes, it is easy to see why walkers regard this corner of the National Park as one of those rare, special places. From Danby Lodge the walk wends its way towards Danby Low Moor before heading south to the edge of Danby village.

Distance: 4 miles/6.5km
Height gain: 315ft/96m
Walking time: 2 hours
Start/Finish: Danby Lodge, east of Danby village. GR717084.
Type of walk: Mostly moorland paths and tracks, with constant, uninterrupted views over moor and dale.

Danby Lodge, a former shooting lodge, is now the headquarters of the North York Moors National Park Centre. This excellent visitor centre provides comprehensive information on the region and includes exhibitions and refreshments. Danby Lodge, with its 13 acres of riverside meadow, ornamental woodland and terraced gardens, is open daily between April and October; weekends only between November and March.

From Danby Lodge turn left and walk up the road. When it bends left towards Danby station and Castleton, go straight on through a gate and up the path between trees. Go through a gate at the top of the rise and head across moorland, keeping a wall on the left. Bear right about 120yds/m before a gate in the corner of the boundary and head down the path between banks of bracken, passing beneath power lines.

Veer right at the fork, cross a stile and footbridge and then turn right to skirt an area of moorland. Ascend the slope, keeping the wall and woodland on the right. Swing right, in line with the wall, absorbing the magnificent view of Esk Dale stretching to the horizon. Whatever the season in the North York Moors, whatever the weather, this is one of those classic panoramas that walkers often stumble upon when they least expect it.

Turn sharp left at the road and follow it as it curves right. Take the next bridleway on the left and follow the track through the heather moorland. This barren, unrelieved landscape forms the walk's backdrop for some time. Eventually the path reaches a boundary fence. Veer right and keep alongside it. On reaching the drive to Clitherbeck Farm, go straight on to the road.

Turn left and follow the unfenced road, pass a footpath and continue to a track on the left, running off through the heather and bracken. Follow the track, known as Lord's Turnpike, and when it forks, about 50yds/m before a drystone wall and gate, keep right. Cross a track and descend between carpets of bracken. Follow the track down to a gate. Ahead is Danby village. Keep the wall on the right, turning sharp left about 50yds/m before a row of cottages.

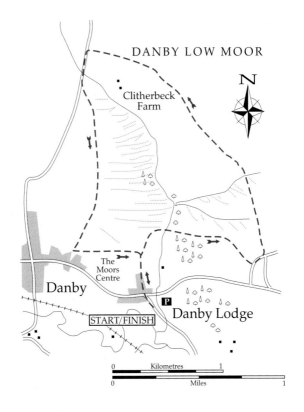

Follow the track through a gate and when it curves left, continue ahead alongside the wall. Make for a gate in the bottom boundary, turn right and take the path down the wooded slope to the road. Danby Lodge and its car park are just ahead.

9 Danby Castle

A short, easy walk through Esk Dale, ideal as an evening stroll or for stretching the legs after a visit to Danby Lodge. The route's main attraction is Danby Castle, occupying a commanding position on the far slopes of Danby Rigg.

Distance: 2¹/₄ miles/3.5km **Height gain:** 211ft/64m **Walking time:** 1-1¹/₄ hours **Start/Finish:** Danby Lodge, east of Danby village. GR717084.	**Type of walk:** Gentle paths and quiet country lanes as far as Danby Castle. The return leg crosses rolling farmland and then follows a stretch of road before reaching Danby Lodge.

Make for the main entrance to Danby Lodge. Avoid entering the grounds; instead, take the path signposted Danby village, following a section of the Esk Valley Walk. Follow the path, glancing to the right for an impressive view of Danby Lodge. On the left sycamores can be seen fringing the parkland. Pass a stile and continue to a footbridge spanning the River Esk. White willow trees, common to river valleys, grow on the bank here; the leaf is narrow and a distinctive silver-grey.

Keep to the path as it curves gently to the right. Make for two kissing gates, with the Middlesbrough to Whitby railway line between

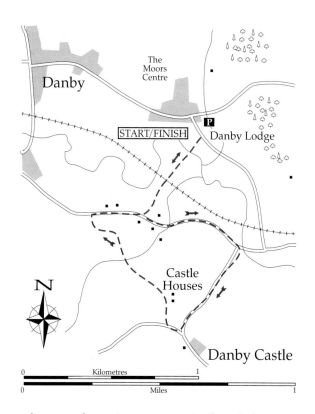

them, and continue on a raised path between hedges and fences.

Turn left at the road and pass over a beck, a tributary of the Esk. Further on, the lane begins to curve right. As it does so, look for the railway track running straight as a plumb line along the dale floor. Continue to Duck Bridge, spanning the river.

This ancient, high-arched packhorse bridge, which dates back to the late-14th century, bears the coat of arms of the de Brus and Latimer families. Repaired in 1715 by George Duck, who was paid the princely sum of ten pounds, seven shillings and sixpence for his trouble, the bridge also includes a Ministry of Works sign dating back to the early part of this century. The sign warns that any person injuring or defacing the monument will be liable to prosecution, according to law.

Do not cross the bridge; instead, stay on the road and follow it towards Danby Castle, seen against the wooded north-facing slopes of Danby Rigg. Pass the entrance to Castle Houses on the right and make for the next road junction, with the castle ruin just a few yards away.

Danby Castle, part of which is a farmhouse, dates back to the late-14th century and was once the home of Catherine Parr, before she became the sixth wife of Henry VIII. The castle is being restored with the help of English Heritage and the North York Moors National Park.

Turn right at the junction and follow the road as far as a footpath sign on the right. Go down the field, keeping the boundary on the right. Draw level with Castle Houses farm outbuildings and cross a stile. Bear left across the field to a ladder-stile in the wall. Cross the field diagonally, making for a kissing gate and footpath sign. Follow the clear path straight up the field to a stile and footpath sign in the top boundary.

Turn left here and walk between fence and hedgerow. Bear right at the kissing gate and continue between hedge and field to the road. Turn right and follow the lane past Kadelands Farm and a sports ground. Bear left just beyond a house on the right and follow the path back to Danby Lodge, seen nestling serenely amid the trees, recrossing the railway line and the river.

Stanley Bond

Ugglebarnby, near Whitby

THE EASTERN MOORS AND HERITAGE COAST

Between Pickering and Scarborough the landscape is cloaked by the trees of the North Riding Forest Park, an area once covered by the ancient Royal Hunting Forest of Pickering. Today, this is the largest upland heath forest in the country, with an extensive network of waymarked paths and woodland rides for visitors to explore and enjoy. Sheltering below Sneaton High Moor, and in sharp contrast to its luxuriant carpet of heather, the densely shaded upper reaches of May Beck offer plenty of opportunity for a gentle stroll between overhanging trees and through tunnels of foliage.

Between Whitby and Scarborough, the hills, moors and dales of the National Park finally give way to the North Sea. Before they do, however, they offer the walker one last opportunity to savour the rare beauty of this regal land.

Fylingdales Moor, blighted only by the undulating ribbon of the busy A171 holiday route, stretches like a purple carpet almost as far as the coast, its sinister MOD tracking station, a permanent focus of curious fascination, incongruously situated at the heart of this stark, heathery landscape. Here, as elsewhere in the National Park, it is possible to walk for miles in complete solitude.

The wonderful sense of space and distance stimulated by tramping the North York Moors is matched only by the liberating experience of exploring the region's spectacular Heritage Coast on foot. Here, the sights and sounds of the sea assault the senses, diverting the attention by laying bare its greatest riches.

Thankfully, the coastline's protected status has enabled it to retain its unique character and culture. Many of the walks in this section make good use of the Cleveland Way's coastal stretches, where towering, steep-sided cliffs spill down to the sea in jumbled assembly and, at their feet, picturesque fishing villages cling for protection in the face of violent storms and pounding waves.

The merciless forces of the sea can never be tamed and erosion has taken its toll on some sections of coastline. As each year passes, more of the crumbling clifftop is destroyed by the elements. Despite the effects of erosion, the cliffs, divided by verdant ravines rich in botanic vegetation and littered with fascinating geological quirks, offer plenty of opportunity for pleasant walking.

Several walks in this section follow stretches of two disused railway lines, which have been adapted for use by those on foot. These recreational linear trails enable walkers to enjoy the local scenery with the minimum of physical effort. The Middlesbrough to Whitby railway, originally commissioned to carry minerals, ran for 75 years, between 1883 and 1958; the Whitby to Scarborough line, popular with holidaymakers and day visitors to the coast, was opened in 1885 and abandoned in 1956.

10 Staithes and Port Mulgrave

Turning off the coast road for Staithes, there is a strong urge to hurry down to this picturesque fishing village, descending the steep streets and alleyways to find the true heart of Staithes. But to do so would be to spoil a diverse walk. Far better to keep this coastal gem until the end. So, instead, the route begins by turning its back on the cliffs and heading for the rolling, semi-wooded countryside around the villages of Roxby and Hinderwell. The scenery is soft and pleasing to the eye and the faint tang of the sea on the breeze a reminder that the coast is never far away.

Distance:
5 miles/8km
Height gain: 220ft/67m
Walking time:
2¾-3 hours
Start/Finish: Staithes.
GR781185. Car park
above the village. No

cars permitted in the
centre of Staithes.
Type of walk: Mainly
undulating field paths,
and a stretch of the
Cleveland Way, ending
with a steep climb out of
Staithes.

From the car park at the top of Staithes walk away from the village to the junction with the A174. Turn right towards Teesside, bearing left very soon for Dalehouse, Roxby and Borrowby. Follow the road round to the right and down between high hedgerows. Leave the road just before the *Fox and Hounds* and join a footpath on the left. Head up the slope for a few strides to a stile, then walk up the field, keeping the fence on the right. Pass through a galvanised gate and continue with the field boundary on the right. The houses of Staithes are visible over to the left. Join a track and continue to maintain the same direction.

Make for a stile and finger post. Turn right and head towards Borrowby, keeping a farm on the right. Cross a track and head down the field, passing under some power lines and aiming slightly right to some trees and bushes in the corner. Keep the fence on the left, cross a stile to some caravans and cross the track to a footbridge. Once over the beck, ascend some steps and bear sharp left up the grassy bank.

Follow a rough, sometimes muddy path through undergrowth, with glimpses of fields on the left. Head up the slope towards a stile by the fence corner. Turn left here to another stile and skirt the field by keeping close to its left-hand boundary. Pass through a wide gap between trees and gorse bushes and head for where the field tapers.

Look for a footbridge, cross it and turn right. Follow the lower slopes of the field, with woodland on the right, and pass to the immediate right of the buildings of Plum Tree Farm. Follow the grassy track to the next junction. Cross the stile on the left and head diagonally across the field. Look for a gap in the hedgerow, about 80 yds/m from the corner of the field. Descend a steep, grassy slope

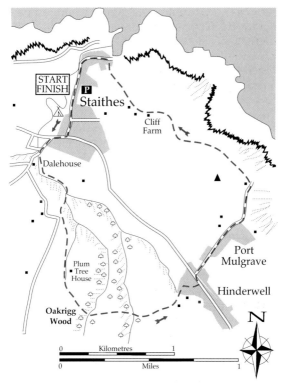

between trees and bushes; bear right on reaching a
junction with a muddy track and go through a
gate, keeping the beck on the left. Follow the leafy
path as it crosses the water, then cuts between the
trees to reach the woodland boundary.

Cross the field to a further area of woodland,
descend some steps to a footbridge, then climb to
higher ground via several stiles. Much of the walk

can be seen from this point, most notably Borrowby Dale and the rolling, well-wooded countryside to the south of Staithes. Join a track and head towards the buildings of Hinderwell. When the track bends left by a cottage, go straight on along a path into the village. Pass a row of houses and merge with the road.

Head straight on to the junction with the A174. Turn left, branching right after about 150yds/m for Port Mulgrave. Follow Rosedale Lane, passing the Ship Inn on the right and a footpath on the left. The sea edges into view now as the road makes for the coast at Port Mulgrave.

Looking at Port Mulgrave today, it is hard to imagine this tiny community was once at the heart of a thriving local industry. During the 19th century the now peaceful cottages and the neglected harbour were an important centre for the extraction and shipment of ironstone. The ironstone, first mined here in 1855, was transported from the mines at Dalehouse by narrow gauge railway, eventually emerging through a tunnel at the foot of the cliff before being shipped north to blast furnaces in Jarrow, where it was later used in shipbuilding.

Work began on building the three-and-a-half-acre harbour at Port Mulgrave in 1856 at a cost of £45,000. Cottages were later built for the local workforce, which was supplemented by labourers brought in from Lincolnshire and Norfolk. Port Mulgrave finally closed in 1930 and though the abandoned pier remains, the Royal Engineers destroyed the breakwater to prevent German forces from invading.

Donald Dakeyne

Staithes

Continue on the road until it terminates and then go forward onto a track, following a stretch of the Cleveland Way. Port Mulgrave's impressive natural setting can be seen in its entirety from the clifftop path. Problems with erosion have led to the Cleveland Way being diverted here, so follow the signs and turn left, briefly heading away from the sea. Cross the field and the path can be seen traversing the headland on its approach to Staithes.

Cross various stiles before reaching Cliff Farm. Keep the farm buildings on the left and head straight on. Pass a sign for Runswick Bay and take the path down into Staithes, the walk's final objective.

First impressions of Staithes are usually favourable. From a distance, it looks so vulnerable, with the waves of the North Sea crashing at its feet, as if clinging to life by a thread. But the village has an indomitable spirit, an instinct for survival. For centuries, this haphazard jumble of quaint cottages has resisted the elements, defying the angry forces of the sea.

The village has changed little over the years, despite the influx of tourists, and looking at the place it is easy to see why James Cook had such a taste for adventure. Before he became one of the world's great navigators, Cook was employed in the village as a grocer's assistant. The quayside shop where he worked for eighteen months was wrecked by violent storms in the 19th century. Materials salvaged from the original shop may have been used in the construction of new premises in Church Street, now known as Cook's Cottage.

Follow the main street past the Captain Cook and Staithes Heritage Centre and climb steeply to the car park at the top of the hill.

11 Saltburn-by-the-Sea

This is a walk of constant delights and surprises. It gets off to a fine start by quickly escaping the bustle of Saltburn, plunging deep into the hushed woodland of the Saltburn Gill Nature Reserve. The playful cries of children on the beach soon fade into the distance as the route cuts through peaceful glades and between great swathes of bracken. Skirting the village of Brotton, the walk explores a mixture of farmland and woodland before joining a stretch of Cleveland Street, a cross-country path running between Guisborough and Skinningrove. The route returns to Brotton, passing through the village centre, and finishes by following the Cleveland Way over remote headland, with magnificent views of the coast en route.

Distance:
8 miles/13km
Height gain:
400ft/122m
Walking time:
3-3¹/₄ hours
Start/Finish: Saltburn-by-the-Sea. GR667215. Car park at eastern end

of the town, signposted Beach and Valley Gardens.
Type of walk: A long tramp through a nature reserve, along field and woodland paths, and on windswept trackways and headland paths.

Saltburn Gill, owned and managed as a nature reserve by the Cleveland Wildlife Trust, is a Site of Special Scientific Interest and contains a wide variety of native trees – oak, ash and elm among them. The reserve also *includes a dense understorey of hazel, hawthorn, holly, blackthorn and honeysuckle. In spring, the woodland floor supports an abundance of dog's mercury, wood anemone and wild garlic. A variety of ferns flourish on the damp valley slopes and Jurassic sandstone can be seen in places. Woodpeckers, warblers and owls are also known to inhabit the area and roe deer can sometimes be spotted in the woods.*

Head for the far end of the car park, cross the bridge and follow the road away from the sea. As it bends to the right at a bridge, turn left to join a footpath, following it over a footbridge. Cross a stile and continue through the nature reserve, beside the Saltburn Gill. Cross several stiles, avoiding paths running off to the left and right and climb some steps.

When the path forks, on the edge of a bracken clearing, keep right and cross a stile by a sign for the nature reserve. Continue between bracken and stands of gorse, with a steep drop on the right. Follow the path for some time, eventually reaching a field. Walk along its right-hand boundary, soon reaching a clear path which cuts across the fields towards the houses of Brotton.

The path widens to a track running between trees, hedges and fencing. On reaching the A173 road, turn right for several steps to a footpath. Drop down the slope to several stiles, then head up a flight of steps through the trees. Once clear of the woodland and undergrowth, curve right and follow the field boundary to another stile. Continue on the path across open fields towards

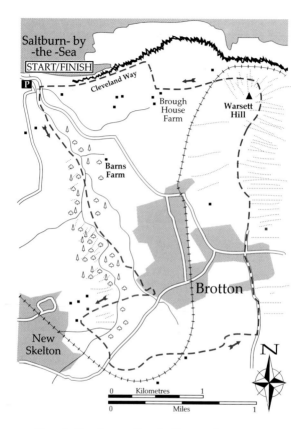

another belt of woodland. Descend some steps between the trees, cross a narrow bridge over the Millholme Beck and climb up the valley slope. When the path forks, keep left and walk between a hedgerow on the left and a grassy bank topped by a fence on the right.

At the next junction, turn left and follow the track as it bends left and right before running down to skirt a field alongside some woodland. The track narrows to a fieldside path, descending gradually towards some trees. Follow the path into the wood, cross a footbridge and head up some steps to the edge of another field. Go straight on, keeping the trees on the right, to pass under some pylons. Turn right at the main road, then left after about 100yds/m. Follow the broad track, part of Cleveland Street, and when it curves right, cross a stile and follow the track across several fields.

Drop down to a footbridge, cut across the field to the next boundary and head up the slope. There are glimpses of the coast at this stage of the walk. Beyond the next stile cross the track beds of two parallel dismantled railway lines and follow the path along the left-hand boundary of a field. On reaching the road, turn left and walk along to the centre of Brotton.

Cross over into Ings Lane, to the right of a Spa shop, and follow the road through a residential area. Turn right at the junction with St Margaret's Way and follow the road. Join the drive leading to Hunley Hall Golf Club. Go straight on at the next junction, pass the clubhouse on the left and turn left immediately beyond it. Curve to the right by some bungalows and follow a track with the green expanse of the fairways and a stunning view of the coastline over to the right. Cross a stile and veer slightly right, soon curving left around the lower flank of Warsett Hill.

This local landmark, acquired by the National Trust in 1991 with the help of various donations and the Enterprise Neptune Fund, is noted for its Bronze Age barrow from which there are some splendid views of the coast and the Cleveland countryside. The only building to be seen here is an old fan house, used for the ventilation of an ironstone mine between 1872 and 1906.

Cross a stile and follow the track. At the next stile, note the arrow engraved, unusually, on the gatepost. Continue to the next stile and the dismantled railway encountered earlier in the walk can be seen here. Pass a National Trust sign for Warsett Hill and follow the path to a stile and gate. Cross the disused trackbed and several more stiles before reaching Brough House Farm. Turn right at this point and head for the Cleveland Way clifftop path. On reaching it, bear left and head towards Saltburn. Pass a line of whitewashed cottages, descend some steps to the road, turn right and return to the car park.

With its dignified air and refined architecture, it is hard to believe the once-fashionable Victorian resort of Saltburn-by-the-Sea lies in the shadow of sprawling, industrial Middlesbrough. The town is situated on a promontory, with one of its most popular walks snaking along the wooded Skelton Beck. Saltburn, which includes Britain's oldest water-balanced cliff railway, marks the start of the Cleveland Way's coastal stretch.

12 Whitby

A coastal walk that makes good use of the trackbed of the disused Whitby to Scarborough railway, as well as a lengthy stretch of the Cleveland Way. From the foot of the famous steps in Whitby, it is an easy roadside amble to the town's outskirts where the route joins the former railway. The trackbed cuts through pleasant countryside, with frequent glimpses of North Yorkshire's hinterland. Beyond the villages of Stainsacre and Hawsker, the walk makes for the Cleveland Way, following it back towards the port of Whitby, with the soaring cliffs and views of the sea forming a constant backdrop.

Distance: *8 miles/13km*	*GR901113.*
Height gain:	***Type of walk:*** *The*
366ft /110m	*railway trackbed gives*
Walking time:	*easy walking, while the*
3½ hours	*final leg traverses a*
Start/Finish: *Whitby.*	*dramatic clifftop.*

Whitby's historic abbey, often lashed by violent storms and howling gales, looks down over the town and its harbour from its commanding position on the East Cliff. The building has suffered greatly over the years; the nave collapsed during a storm in 1763, and the central tower experienced the same fate in 1830. The abbey also became the subject of enemy bombardment when German warships attacked it during the First World War. The adjacent church of St Mary is closely associated with

Count Dracula. Bram Stoker's classic tale refers to the graveyard as being one of Dracula's haunts. The church's dramatic, clifftop setting, overlooking the harbour, makes it an obvious choice for inclusion in a work of fiction.

From the foot of the 199 steps leading up to the remains of Whitby Abbey, head south to the junction with Bridge Street. To explore the town fully, turn right and cross the swing bridge spanning the River Esk.

The Esk divides both Whitby and its character. The eastern side of the river consists of quaint old streets and inns with windows overlooking the harbour, while across the water lies the busy quayside, overlooked by fish restaurants and amusement arcades. This corner of the town throngs with visitors and holidaymakers during the season. Up above these bustling streets lie rows of Georgian houses, most of which are hotels and holiday apartments, giving this part of Whitby the air of a genteel seaside resort.

It is here that the town's famous Whale Arch can be seen, a reminder of Whitby's former whaling industry. Near it stands the Captain Cook Monument, with a statue of the great man gazing wistfully out to sea. It was here in Whitby that James Cook learned his craft. Twice during 1997, the working replica of the navigator's pioneering ship Endeavour made historic visits to this famous port, witnessed by large crowds on the quayside.

Return to the swing bridge and follow Church Street to the A171. Cross over into Larpool Lane, passing the *Oak Tree Inn*. The unmistakable outline of a railway viaduct edges into view on the right. Pass a cemetery, its ornate arch adding a final touch of grace and beauty to this peaceful burial ground. Glancing back at this point reveals a striking view of Whitby Abbey and the neighbouring parish church on the clifftop above the town. Pass the entrance to Larpool Hall, a country house hotel, on the left and continue along the road to the railway bridge.

Pass under the bridge and bear immediately right. Ascend the bank to the disused trackbed and turn right. The facade of Larpool Hall can be seen on the left. Over to the right are the church and buildings of the village of Ruswarp. Follow the trackbed, with glimpses here and there of distant rolling moorland and tracts of open countryside. Further on, a footpath can be seen running under the line of the former railway. Continue on the path and soon the houses of Stainsacre come into view up ahead. On the left are the buildings of Hall Farm. Follow the path above a road leading into the village and keep going to the next road bridge.

The path, enclosed now by trees and bushes, runs close to the A171 as far as Hawsker, the next village. Up ahead is the building of the former railway station, now a private house and the offices of a cycle hire company. Follow the path to the right of it and head for a gate leading out to the main road. Cross over and continue on the next stretch of trackbed, passing under a bridge. Follow the path between open fields, with teasing glimpses of the cliffs and the North Sea. The Cleveland Way, the

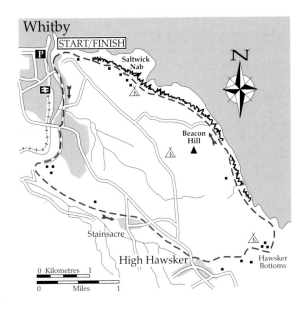

walk's next objective, can be seen running along the clifftop towards Whitby.

On reaching a junction, by some caravans, leave the former railway by turning left and following the lane between hedgerows. Bear round to the right, pass a sign for North Cliff Holiday Park, cross Oakham Beck, prettily enclosed by trees far below, and veer right at a waymark. Turn left at the next footpath sign, keep right at the fork and walk down between rows of caravans towards the sea. Further down, as the route approaches a gate, veer off half left to a path. Cross the grass and descend the slope to join the Cleveland Way. Turn left at the sign and drop down to the Oakham Beck, crossing it close to where it flows into the sea at Maw Wyke Hole. Climb up the slope and follow the Cleveland Way towards Whitby, keeping the fence and sea on the immediate right.

Drop down to a stile and then ascend a flight of steps, enclosed by a tunnel of trees. On reaching the higher ground once more, pass a footpath on the left. Drop down to another beck and stile via steps. Go upslope and look back for a stunning view of the coast, including Maw Wyke Hole. Pass a Cleveland Way sign (follow path to lighthouse), and follow the path alongside the boundary wall of the lighthouse to a stile. Cross a private road and take the Cleveland Way diagonally down-field to the old Whitby Fog Signal. Cross the ladder-stile and keep to the right of the building to another stile.

Continue on the Cleveland Way, and soon the ruined abbey and the outskirts of the town loom into view below the horizon. Glancing to the right reveals a splendid view of the coastline, particularly at low tide when the shifting sea exposes a fascinating, intricately-detailed maze of haphazard mudflats, fossils and sculptured rock pools.

Cross several more stiles before reaching a caravan park on the edge of Whitby. Pass a turning down to the seashore and continue between the buildings of the holiday site. When the drive bends left, go straight on along the path, passing a National Trust sign for Saltwick Nab. There are good views here down to Saltwick Bay and the famously narrow entrance to Whitby harbour can be seen jutting out into the North Sea beyond the next headland.

Follow the clear path past the former coastguard look-out, now a derelict and abandoned building staring forlornly into the vastness of the North Sea. Owing to the instability of the cliff face beneath the footpath, the Cleveland Way turns left now and heads away from the sea, towards the abbey remains. Turn right at the road and follow it to the car park and the entrance to the abbey. With St Mary's church over to the right, walk down past the youth hostel to the flight of 199 steps and return to the centre of Whitby.

Whitby

Donald Dakeyne

13 Hackness

With its collection of fine buildings and canalised stream running beneath an ornamental bridge, Hackness makes a perfect starting point for this superb walk which explores the secret valleys and dales to the north of the village. The romantically-named Whisper Dales, characterised by undisturbed pastures and swathes of conifer plantations, is a great favourite with walkers. To the south lies Low Dales and here the walk climbs steeply through trees to provide a window on this splendid, rolling landscape.

Distance: *8 miles/13km*	***Type of walk:*** *A moderate walk that explores Hackness before climbing to Broxa, where an undulating path enters wooded valleys and dales.*
Height gain: *210ft/64m*	
Walking time: *2¹/₂ -3 hours*	
Start/Finish: *Hackness car park. GR968911.*	

From the car park turn right and follow the lane, carefully negotiating the hairpin bends down to the junction in Hackness village centre. The church is a short walk to the left.

The estate village of Hackness dates back to AD 680 when St Hilda, Abbess of Whitby, dispatched a group of monks and nuns to establish a small monastery here. Nearly 200 years later, the settlement fell victim to pillaging Danes. The present church includes a Saxon cross bearing inscriptions in Latin, Anglo-Saxon and ogam, an ancient form of Irish alphabet. Hackness Hall, an imposing late 18th century house designed by John Carr of York, was the home of the 17th century diarist, Lady Elizabeth Hoby. Part of the house was destroyed by fire at the beginning of this century. Today, Hackness Hall, which is not open to the public, is the family seat of Lord Derwent.

Bear right and follow the road round the left-hand bend, passing a turning on the right to Low Dales and High Dales. Keep going on the pavement and look for a track running off half right up the bank. Follow it as it curves to the right, rising steeply through a tunnel of trees. Keep right at the fork and continue to climb, with glorious views providing glimpses of the River Derwent and the trees of the 3,300-acre Wykeham Forest in the distance.

Enter a field and continue ahead, keeping the fence and trees on the left. Pass a reassuring waymark and begin to veer a little to the right, following the ridge of the field to a gate. Aim for the right-hand edge of the next field. Cross several field boundaries, hard by a curtain of trees, and continue towards Broxa Farm. When the farm comes into view, the path leaves the woodland boundary and heads diagonally across the field to reach a metal gate and stile in front of the outbuildings.

Head straight on to the road and turn right. Follow the lane between hedgerows and when it begins to curve left towards a line of trees, bear right at a

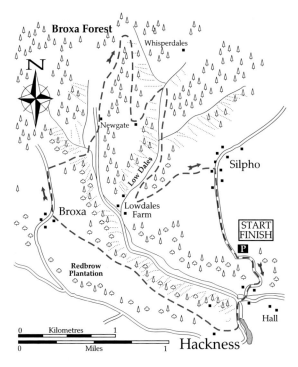

stile. Walk down the field to Fewler Gate Wood. The next stage of the walk can be overgrown in places during the summer months, though the path is not impenetrable.

Progress down through trees, eventually reaching a fence on the edge of the woodland. Turn right and follow the field edge to a stile on the right. Do not cross it; instead, aim to the left of a gateway in the bottom boundary and follow the western bank of the beck, keeping it close by on the right. Cross a footbridge leading to Newgate Farm, turn left at the track and look for a gate on the right, following the bridle path up the slope through trees. Pass through a gate, cross a track and continue ahead through woodland.

Follow the path round to the right and bear right at the next junction by some larch trees and clumps of heather. Head south on a clear track and look for glimpses of Whisper Dales between the trees on the left. Pass a gate, with a sign for Heights Farm, and continue between trees, gorse bushes and carpets of heather. On reaching a signposted junction, turn left for Whisper Dales and walk down the field.

Make for a semi-enclosed area of bracken and trees, the path descending quite steeply along a ledge. The ground falls away abruptly between trees on the right. Curve to the right at the foot of the slope and continue through the foliage, alongside a fence. On reaching a field, look away to the left for a splendid view of Whisper Dales, enclosed by thickly afforested slopes cloaked with conifers. Cross the field diagonally to reach a bridleway.

Turn right and follow the track towards Low Dales. The tree-clad escarpment of Haggland Wood, the walk's next objective, rises dramatically in the distance. Go through several gates, the scarp looming above the walk like a slumbering giant. Take the bridleway on the left, just beyond Low Dales Cottage, and follow it as it snakes round the field and up the grassy hillside. Pass through a gate and traverse the escarpment. From here, there is a magnificent view of Low Dales stretching as far as Whisper Dales.

Continue the steep pull and then bear left at the top. Follow the track as it runs alongside arable land and round to the right. Now enclosed by trees and bushes, the track curves to the left and right before reaching the road at Silpho. Turn right and follow the lane. Pass the old Methodist chapel, dated 1900, and Binkleys Farm Cottage and continue along the road, back to the car park. This final stretch of the walk offers fine views in all directions.

Robin Hood's Bay

14 Robin Hood's Bay

With its moorland views, stretches of disused railway track and secret smuggler haunts, this richly varied walk offers something for everyone. Heading south from Robin Hood's Bay on a section of the Whitby to Scarborough trackbed, the route explores tracts of rolling, high-level countryside on the edge of Fylingdales Moor. The coastal views become ever more spectacular as the walk makes for the Cleveland Way, following the cliff path to Boggle Hole and on to Bay Town.

Distance: 8 miles/13km
Height gain:
395ft/120m
Walking time:
3½ hours
Start/Finish: Robin
Hood's Bay. GR951055.

Car park opposite
Mount Pleasant North.
Type of walk: The route
uses a lengthy, easy
section of the former
Whitby to Scarborough
railway, and field paths.

The upper part of Robin Hood's Bay, comprising hotels, guest houses and holiday flats, has fallen victim to intensive development over the years; the true village, at the foot of the hill and known on this stretch of the coast as Bay Town, began as a fishing community way back in the 1500s. Consisting of a network of narrow streets, alleyways and picture-postcard buildings, Bay Town was once one of the most prosperous fishing villages in the area, with more than 130 fishermen living here. Cod, lobster, herring and crab were all caught from shallow fishing boats known as 'cobles'.

The introduction of high taxes in the 18th century made smuggling a profitable and common occupation in coastal villages and Bay Town was no exception. Rum, brandy, tobacco, tea and silk were brought to these shores from Holland and France. Gangs of smugglers used a network of underground passages and secret tunnels to bring the booty ashore. According to legend, Robin Hood visited this stretch of coast, helping to repel Danish invaders.

From the car park, keep to the left of the former station building and follow a lane (signposted: *Railway Path*). Bear right at the road and when it swings right, turn left and continue on the next section of the disused trackbed. Robin Hood's Bay can be seen over to the left. Pass some silos and a campsite at Middlewood Farm and keep going between trees and margins of foliage. Go straight on at the next road, pass under a stone railway bridge and look for glimpses of the North Sea through trees and gateways and between hedges.

Turn right on reaching the next road, follow it to the right and then bear left to join a bridleway leading to Swallow Head Farm. Pass through a gate and look back for a magnificent view of Robin Hood's Bay, with a vast, unrelieved seascape stretching to the horizon. Go through another gate, veer left at the fork and follow the bridleway between gorse bushes. The track curves to the right, then left by a right of way sign and a hawthorn tree.

Make for a gate, cross a stile and follow the track. Pass a gateway on the right and when the track

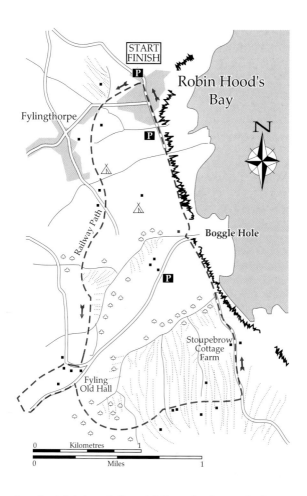

bends right, turn left and follow the footpath down the field, keeping the boundary close by on the right. Skirt several fields and when a house comes into view up ahead, veer to the left of it and exit from the field through the gate.

Turn left, pass Colcroft Farm and follow the country lane between hedgerows and trees. Just beyond a solitary cottage and a footpath, the walk rejoins the disused railway track. Take the path on the left, immediately before the bridge, and follow it down through the trees. Turn right and follow the old trackbed, pleasantly shaded here by trees. On the right are glimpses of open moorland.

Pass under the next bridge, the former line running high above peaceful hollows and wooded denes. Beyond the next bridge, the path provides views over a variety of scenery, including glimpses of Robin Hood's Bay. Pass Browside Farm on the right; the farm track crosses the railway at this point and some of the original sleepers can still be seen today. Cut between gorse bushes, and now the path curves imperceptibly to the right, climbing gently towards the next bridge.

Once under it, bear left to the road. Turn right and follow the lane down to Stoupebrow Cottage Farm, absorbing en route one of the grandest and most memorable views of Robin Hood's Bay. On reaching Stoupe Bank Farm, join the Cleveland Way and follow the path through the undergrowth. Cross Stoupe Beck via the footbridge. A small, sheltered beach can be seen just a few yards away on the right. At low tide, it is possible to return to Robin Hood's Bay along the shore.

To avoid the beach, climb back to the cliff top via a stepped path and pass a National Trust sign for Boggle Hole. Take the steps down to this sheltered ravine, famous for its superbly situated youth hostel, once a corn mill and a refuge for shipwrecked sailors, overlooking the bay. Cross the footbridge over Mill Beck and return to the clifftop.

Many signs urge walkers not to stray from the path on this next stretch as this is private land. The houses of Robin Hood's Bay, consisting of the old quarter down by the sea and the more modern development above it, can be clearly seen ahead now. Pass through a kissing gate and then follow a stretch of boardwalk. Descend steps under the trees and walk into the centre of Bay Town.

The Bay Hotel includes the Coast to Coast Bar, named after the 190-mile/305km long-distance path which officially terminates here. Badges and certificates are available for those who complete the route. Walk away from the sea and follow the street lined with shops and cafes. Climb steeply out of Bay Town and pass an old naval mine used during the Second World War in the defence of this coast and as a defensive weapon in enemy waters. Cross the roundabout, pass the Victoria Hotel and return to the upper car park.

15 Runswick Bay

Runswick Bay, a picturesque jumble of multicoloured cottages huddled at the foot of the cliffs, overlooks one of the loveliest bays on the Yorkshire coast. The walk climbs steeply out of the village to the disused Middlesbrough to Whitby railway, now a pleasantly leafy permitted path that sweeps round expansively to Kettleness, and provides teasing glimpses of the North Sea. Leaving the railway path, the route heads for a wide curve of cliff, joining a scenic stretch of the Cleveland Way as it approaches Runswick Bay. Winding its way precipitously down to the beach, the walk finishes with a gentle stroll on the sands.

Distance: 5½ miles/9km	park is just a few yards from the beach.
Height gain: 341ft/105m	**Type of walk:** A steep climb away from the sea
Walking time: 2½-3 hours	and a spell on the road lead to the disused
Start/Finish: Runswick Bay. GR808158: the car	trackbed of the Loftus to Whitby line.

The placid scene at Runswick Bay on a summer's day belies its disastrous past. It was in 1682 that the original village slipped into the sea, though fortunately no lives were lost. The new village is characterised by the red roofs of its pretty cottages, and the lifeboat station here is a constant reminder of the perilous nature of this coast. In 1901, with their husbands at sea, the women of

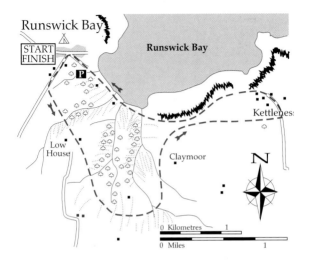

Runswick Bay distinguished themselves by launching the lifeboat during a violent storm.

In his memoirs, James Herriot recalls a very enjoyable weekend spent with his family in Runswick Bay many years ago, though the steepness of the main street made him more than a little anxious as he approached the village by car. A new road has since been built, but in those days the approach into Runswick Bay was almost a sheer drop.

From the car park follow the road as it climbs steeply out of Runswick Bay. Turn left at the top, by the Runswick Bay Hotel, into Ellerby Lane. Pass a row of houses on the right before reaching the village sign for Runswick Bay. Bear left about 60 yds/m beyond it, through a gap in the hedgerow, head up the bank and join the route of the long-

Runswick Bay

abandoned Middlesbrough to Whitby railway. The narrow path can be quite overgrown in places during the summer months, with a luxuriant curtain of undergrowth either side of it.

Follow the path to the road at Ellerby Crossing Cottage. The sea can just be glimpsed here. Continue ahead on what is now a clearly-defined track. Pass through some gates and under several bridges on the former railway. The broad expanse of Runswick Bay edges into view and, at one point, the Cleveland Way, the return leg of this walk, is just a stone's throw to the left. Follow the track to the next road and turn left by the old railway buildings.

Follow the lane through Kettleness, with the sea over to the right. Join the route of the Cleveland Way and skirt the buildings of Kettleness Farm, keeping to the right of them. Follow the track to the right, passing a wooden chalet to reach a stile. Cross it and head back towards the cliffs, scene of many shipwrecks over the years, dropping down a flight of steps, then returning to the higher ground. Continue on the clear, grassy path and pass a gate on the left, where a path runs up to the former railway featured earlier in the walk.

The Cleveland Way edges ever closer to the buildings of Runswick Bay. Make for a flight of steps, taking you down to the bay. Follow the path by the beck and then head along the beach to the village. If time allows, explore the fascinating maze of back alleys and picturesque passageways which help to give Runswick Bay its unique character.

16 Ravenscar and Hayburn Wyke

Anyone who makes a study of geology and botany will immediately be drawn to the natural attractions of this splendid coastal walk, which begins by exploring a corner of the North York Moors National Park once considered ripe for commercial exploitation. However, plans to transform the area into one seamless chain of holiday resorts never reached fruition and today, thankfully, this stretch of coastline survives more or less intact.

> **Distance:** 8 miles/13km
> **Height gain:** 620ft/188m
> **Walking time:** 3½ hours
> **Start/Finish:** Ravenscar. GR978014: roadside parking.
> **Type of walk:** Agreeable walking along a former railway track precedes a clifftop climb; sections are open and exposed to all weathers.

From the roadside parking area head down the road towards the sea, turning right into Station Road by the entrance to the Raven Hall Hotel.

Overlooking a broad sweep of Robin Hood's Bay, Ravenscar is a scattered community that has a sadly neglected air about it, as if it has been bypassed by time, curiously overlooked by the rest of the world: forgotten.

It was back in the 1890s that a development company chose this village, originally called Peak, as the site for a sizable seaside resort that, had it been completed, would probably have rivalled Scarborough in size and status.

Detailed plans of shops, hotels and houses were swiftly drawn up, 400 men were taken on to build roads and drains and Peak soon changed its name to Ravenscar, in an attempt to make its image more appealing. However, a myriad of unforeseen problems, not least of which was the failure to sell most of the plots, led to the project being shelved and today Ravenscar remains much as it was 100 years ago. The 18th century Raven Hall Hotel, built on the site of a Roman signal station, marks the eastern extremity of the Lyke Wake Walk.

Follow the road past a sign for the Cleveland Way. There are good views from here over a rural landscape bordering the coast. Occasional holiday villas and remote farmsteads can be seen dotted about the countryside. On reaching Foxcliffe Tearooms, part of a large building which was a hotel in the days when efforts were being made to establish Ravenscar as a popular seaside resort, veer slightly right by a rectangular green and head for a track, Loring Road. The remains of Ravenscar's former railway station can be seen here and the tearooms sell postcards depicting the hotel and station in 1907.

When the track bends to the right, cross a stile and join the trackbed of the disused Scarborough to Whitby line. Follow the path between margins of vegetation and wild flowers. The ridge of the North York Moors can be seen defining the far horizon. The buildings of Bell Hill Farm can be seen over to the right, amid a rolling landscape of fields, woodland and moorland. Further on, trees and banks of undergrowth begin to close in on either side of the track, providing welcome shade on a warm day. Go through several gates, with Bees Nest Farm over to the right.

Pass a junction of paths and keep ahead, passing through a gate with a sign which reads *Cyclists slow please – children playing*. Walk alongside a cottage and sloping garden and pass the remains of an old station platform, now part of a private house and garden. This used to be Staintondale station. Look for the station clock set in the wall, a relic from the days when the scene here would have looked very different, with the arrival and departure of steam trains creating a flurry of activity.

Continue on the track, following it through woodland and under several stone bridges. Soon the sea can be glimpsed between the trees on the left – a taste of what is to come on this varied walk. Pass through a wooden gate by a house and follow the track to the next road. Leave the railway track at this point; turn left and head down the lane towards the Hayburn Wyke Hotel. Bear sharp right just before the hotel and follow the track to a gate and stile. Veer half left across the field and take the stile into the woods.

During the Victorian era, regular excursions from places like York and Scarborough brought people to explore Hayburn Wyke's woodland and take tea at the local hotel. Up until the early 1960s, visitors arrived by train

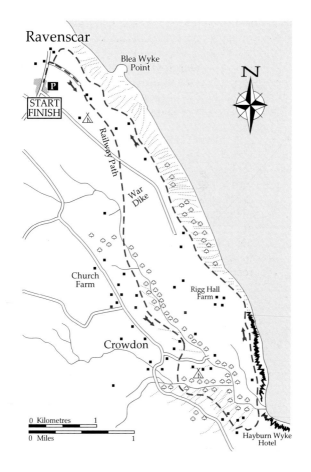

Ravenscar

Blea Wyke
Point

N

START
FINISH

Railway Path

War
Dike

Church
Farm

Rigg Hall
Farm

Crowdon

0 Kilometres 1

0 Miles 1

Hayburn Wyke
Hotel

at Hayburn Wyke station. Many came to study the rich
variety of flora and fauna and to look for evidence of
ferns, fossils and mosses that were growing here 150
million years ago.

Hayburn Wyke is a secluded wooded valley where two streams unite and cascade down to the sea over a series of waterfalls. 'Wyke' is a local term for a small inlet of the sea. The cliffs overlooking the pocket beach are covered with trees, a mixture of oak woodland, native hardwoods and conifer plantations. The area is a rich habitat for birds and the streams and waterfall are a favourite haunt of wagtails in summer.

Follow the path for about 25yds/m to a junction, turn left and descend the steps, following the walk through this glorious woodland. A superbly-sited bench provides a breathtaking view of Hayburn Wyke and the coast. Follow the path parallel to the sea and on reaching a sign for the Cleveland Way, turn right towards the beach. Cross the footbridge and take the stepped path up the cliff. Pass a sign for Staintondale and continue on the Cleveland Way.

Climb steeply and when the path emerges from the trees and foliage, follow it ahead as it skirts open fields, keeping the cliff edge a short distance to the right. This stretch of the walk offers some of the finest views anywhere on the Heritage Coast. Glancing back, the fretted edge of the shoreline can be seen disappearing away to the south beyond Hayburn Wyke.

Continue on the Cleveland Way; at times the view of the sea is obscured by trees and undergrowth. Pass a footpath leading to War Dike Lane and the disused railway line; keep ahead on the coastal path, with views down to the verdant undercliff on the right. Pass an old coastguard lookout and a

Nissen hut on the left and note how the destructive forces of the sea have undermined the cliff on this stretch. The buildings of Ravenscar come into view now. Pass a National Trust sign and ahead is the outline of the Raven Hall Hotel. Just before it, the path turns left and heads inland to the road. Turn right and return to the start.

17 Forge Valley and Raincliffe Woods

Following the woodland paths and tracks through the Raincliffe Woods, it is hard to believe that this walk is so close to Scarborough. At length, the walk climbs out of the woodland and cuts across farmland to the north of East Ayton. There is an optional detour to the village; the main walk, however, heads north on the homeward stretch, tracing a course that runs high above the tree-clad slopes of the Forge Valley.

Distance: 6 miles/9.6km	Gate car park, Raincliffe
Height gain:	Woods. GR985875.
382ft/116m	**Type of walk:** A
Walking time:	delightfully scenic walk
3-3½ hours	on clear, firm tracks and
Start/Finish: Green	paths.

Look for the metal gate and take the track, known as Middle Road, up through trees, following it left after a few yards. Pass a picnic area and keep to the cinder track.

Breaks in the trees on the left reveal Sir George Cayley's 19th century Sea Cut. This hand-dug drain, a feat of engineering by any standards, was designed and excavated to divert flood water from the River Derwent to the sea at Scalby Ness, north of Scarborough.

Make for another picnic area, which also includes a map of Raincliffe Woods, and continue through the mixed woodland. Bear right when the track forks and head for a stile. Cross a tree-lined field and continue through the woods. Keep right at the next fork, by a clump of beech trees and a picnic area, following the path between bracken and undergrowth.

When the path forks by a bench, bear right and climb the slope, merging with another path further up. Cross over at the next junction and follow the path through the crops, sweeping away to the left to reach a cinder track. Turn right and continue in a south-westerly direction.

Pass some barns and sheds and keep going to a junction. Bear right and follow the track, skirting a wood. Make for a gate at the corner of the woodland, turn left here and follow the path along the field boundary.

Aim for a gap in the corner and continue on the enclosed path, rather overgrown in places during the summer months. On reaching a junction by a wood, turn right and follow the bridleway as it cuts through the trees to reach the road. To visit the village of East Ayton turn left.

East Ayton, separated from neighbouring West Ayton by the River Derwent, lies at the entrance to the Vale of Pickering. The remains of ruined Ayton Castle, dating from the 13th century reign of King John and stronghold of the Evers family, can be seen near the river.

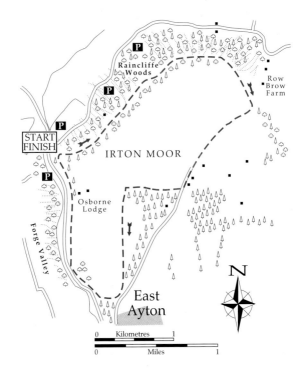

To continue the walk, turn right, heading through the Forge Valley to the next footpath sign on the right. The path can be seen running off half right into the trees.

The steep-sided Forge Valley, through which runs the River Derwent, was cut by melting ice water towards the end of the last Ice Age. These 6,000-year-old deciduous woodlands form a link with the ancient wildwood which once covered much of England. The valley takes its name from the 14th century iron forges which were fuelled by charcoal made in the surrounding woods and worked by the monks of Rievaulx Abbey.

Oak trees can be seen on the upper slopes of the valley, while ash, elm, alder and willow are to be found on the lower flank and close to the river. During the spring and early summer months dog's mercury and primrose are among the many woodland plants to be seen here. The trees are home to a wide variety of birds all year round. Woodpeckers, robins and willow and wood warblers make their home here and a quiet stroll in this area may reveal a nuthatch or a tree creeper searching tree trunks for insects.

Head up the slope, avoiding a path running off to the left, and keep left when the path forks further up the hillside. Follow the path along the woodland perimeter, with good views over open fields to the right. Pass some stone barns and farm outbuildings and keep to the path. On reaching a gate and footpath on the right, veer slightly left and begin to drop down the slope into the gloriously wooded Forge Valley. Follow the path back to the car park at Green Gate.

18 Skinningrove and Hummersea Scar

A blustery coastal walk which begins by climbing above the rooftops of Skinningrove, a sleepy village with a fascinating industrial heritage, and then crosses windswept farmland to reach the Cleveland Way.

Distance: 5 miles/8km
Height gain: 613ft/187m
Walking time: 2 hours
Start/Finish: Skinningrove. GR713202.

Type of walk: Field paths, tracks and several stretches of country road form the outward leg of this breezy walk. The homeward stretch is by coastal, clifftop path.

Skinningrove began life as a mining community, accommodating the men who mined the Cleveland ironstone during the 18th and 19th centuries. The mines have long gone but the Tom Leonard Mining Museum, at the southern end of the village, resonates with the memory of Skinningrove's industrial past. Today, the village is a haphazard jumble of dilapidated shacks, huts and little terraced houses overlooking a small harbour and beach littered with rotting boats and tractors.

If it hadn't been for the scars of local industry, development companies would no doubt have transformed Skinningrove into a thriving holiday village. It is probably just as well that its commercial potential has always been flawed. In a curious way, Skinningrove's obvious decline and air of neglect somehow add to its appeal.

From the car park overlooking the sea, walk along Marine Terrace, turning right into High Street. Pass the Methodist church on the left and bear left by Timms coffee house. When the road bends left, go straight on across the bridge and up a flight of crumbling steps alongside a fence. Keep climbing out of the narrow valley, cross a stile and continue on the grassy path.

Head towards the buildings of Skinningrove Farm, bearing right to a stile just before them. Continue along the field boundary to the next stile, maintain the same direction as far as some fence posts and look for a stile to the right of them, about 30yds/m ahead. Follow the field edge to a track and turn left. Make for the buildings of Deepdale Farm, crossing a stile just before the road.

Turn right and follow the lane to the far end of North Terrace. Bear left at this point to follow a track almost as far as the amusingly-named Downdinner Hill Farm. Turn right at the stile and skirt the field towards Rose Hill Farm. Pass under some pylons and cross three stiles in quick succession at the farm.

The route of the path is clearly waymarked here. Walk down the drive and when it curves right, turn left between the barns and stone outbuildings. Pass through a gate, bear left and

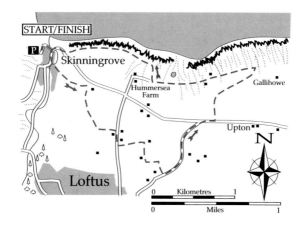

when the track forks after several yards, veer right and head up to a stile to the right of a gate in the top boundary.

Bear right, hugging the field edge as far as a stile leading out to the road. Turn left and follow the lane between the hedgerows, curving to the right by a seat. Keep right at the next junction and take the next footpath on the left. Follow the field boundary, cross a stile and bear right, with the sea clearly in view on this stretch of the walk. Make for another stile, cutting between gorse bushes and a stone wall.

Turn sharp left at the next stile to join the route of the Cleveland Way, following it back towards Skinningrove. Cross several stiles, the route of the walk visible ahead as it runs over the headland. Join a track by a cottage and follow it towards

Hummersea Farm, passing a National Trust sign. Bear right about 200yds/m before the farm and take the grassy track to a sign *Hummersea Beach – uneven steps*. Follow the headland path above Hummersea Scar.

Carved into the flat rocks of Hummersea Scar is a curious, man-made channel originally designed to enable boats to negotiate a precipitous passage between the rocks and load up with alum, which was mined extensively along this coast between 1600 and 1870.

Pass a sign for the Cleveland Way, perched close to the cliff edge. The houses of Skinningrove creep into view now; keep the fence on the left and descend some steps to the road. This unsheltered stretch of the route, approaching the village, can be exceptionally blustery. Turn left at the foot of the stairs, cross the bridge and bear right by some children's swings. Walk along the seafront and back to the car park.

THE CLEVELAND AND HAMBLETON HILLS

The escarpment of the Cleveland and Hambleton Hills represents the North York Moors National Park's western extremity. It may be a political boundary, but the rim of these hills perfectly illustrates the sharp contrast between the rugged, steeply rising scarp and the flat-topped moorland to the east, and the vastness of the fertile Vale of York stretching away under huge skies to the west. This lofty range of windswept hills offers some of the finest walking anywhere in the National Park.

One of the great geological landmarks of the

Donald Dakeyne

Great Ayton and Roseberry Topping

Cleveland Hills is Roseberry Topping, a 1,056ft (322m) conical peak sometimes described as Cleveland's 'Matterhorn'.

Reminiscent of a Roman nose from some angles, and a shark's fin from others, Roseberry Topping has long been a major draw for walkers, who regularly make the climb to enjoy the magnificent views from its summit.

Rising to more than 1,500ft (457m), the Cleveland range still bears the scars of its industrial past, when this area played a key role in the mining of alum and jet. The high tops of Cold Moor, Cringle Moor and Carlton Bank are prime examples.

Along the western escarpment, the Cleveland Way coincides with the old Hambleton Drove Road, part of a network of ancient routes established before the Roman Occupation and once regularly used by shepherds and cattle drovers. Today, the old drove road is the sole preserve of local ramblers and long-distance walkers, following in the footsteps of pedlars, packhorse men and monks. Black Hambleton, which rises to 1,309ft (399m), signifies the highest point of the Hambleton Hills.

South of Black Hambleton, the National Park's perimeter is defined by Sutton Bank, the western gateway to the North York Moors and a notoriously steep ascent for motorists. From the summit, the views over the Vale of York to the Yorkshire Dales and beyond are tremendous. The wooded country in the National Park's south-west corner conceals a string of picturesque villages;

among them Kilburn, sheltering at the foot of the famous White Horse, and Ampleforth, which sits on a shelf of the Hambleton Hills.

19 Captain Cook's Monument

Great Ayton marks the starting point of this spectacular walk, which climbs, steeply in places, through plantations to reach the Captain Cook monument on Easby Moor. Looking out over distant horizons, the monument can be seen from miles around, acting as a useful landmark for those exploring the area on foot. The walk then follows a stretch of the Cleveland Way before dropping down to Little Ayton, Great Ayton's near neighbour.

Distance:	GR561105.
7 miles/11km	**Type of walk:** *Starting*
Height gain:	*with a spell on the road,*
745ft/227m	*the walk climbs towards*
Walking time:	*Easby Moor. There is a*
3½ hours	*steep ascent before the*
Start/Finish: *Great*	*walk descends to Little*
Ayton tourist	*Ayton via forest paths*
information centre.	*and field tracks.*

Captain Cook spent his formative years in the village of Great Ayton, attending the local school which now houses the Captain Cook Schoolroom Museum. Aspects of Cook's early life and his famous voyages are recorded in the museum, which also depicts Great Ayton as Cook would have known it in the 18th century. Members of the great navigator's family are buried in the village churchyard.

From the tourist information centre turn right and then immediately right again into Station Road. Follow the road to Great Ayton railway station, which provides glimpses of Captain Cook's monument standing out on Easby Moor. Pass the station building, cross the railway line and bear right by *Overbridge*, a chalet bungalow. Go through a gate and continue on the track, curving right over a beck. Turn left at the next stile and follow the track to a junction.

Bear right and soon the metalled lane dwindles to a stony path running between banks of undergrowth. Roseberry Topping's bare, conical summit is seen over to the left, against the skyline. Follow the path up alongside the trees of Round Hill. Pass through a gate and continue between gorse bushes and bracken. The line of the Cleveland Hills, denoted by the awesome escarpments of Hasty Bank and Urra Moor, can be seen away to the right.

On reaching the corner of the wall, by the edge of a plantation, turn left to a junction of paths. Veer slightly right, pass over a track and begin the steep, wearisome climb through the trees. Further up, the path bends to the right to reach the edge of Easby Moor.

The inscription on the Captain Cook monument proclaims that "the name of Captain Cook will stand out among the most celebrated and most admired benefactors

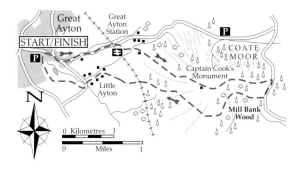

of the human race." The monument, a symbol of admiration and respect for the great explorer, was erected in 1827 by Robert Campion of Whitby and restored in 1895 by the readers of the North Eastern Daily Gazette.

On reaching the granite monument, curve left and follow the Cleveland Way to the right of woodland. Take the paved path down beside the trees, keep right at the fork and head for a junction with a track. There is a sign here for the Cleveland Way. Keep right and follow the track to the road. Turn right and head down the hill. Look for a gate and bridleway sign on the right, just before the road bends left by Bankside Cottage.

There is another sign here: *motorcycles prohibited – keep dogs on a lead.* Follow the bridleway through trees and keep right when the track eventually forks. Cross a boundary wall and pass a path on the left, running down to Borough Green Farm. Continue beside a drystone wall and between margins of invasive bracken to reach a gate leading into a wood.

On reaching a gate in the next boundary, join a path which initially runs down alongside the wall. Avoid a path on the right and descend through the bracken, curving right further down the slope. Continue on the path for some time, disregarding branch turnings, and eventually it reaches a gate and waymark. Cross a track, followed by the route of the Middlesbrough to Whitby railway.

Skirt the field and on reaching a track, by the fence corner, turn right and strike out across farmland. Approach Brookside Farm, turning left here to follow the lane. Bear left, cross the River Leven and swing right to a footpath sign. Cross the field, keeping the fence over to the left, and head towards trees. On reaching the fence corner, veer left and go diagonally across the next field to a stile in the far corner.

Follow the path to the next boundary and continue alongside the hedge. Skirt Great Ayton's sports ground and the spire of the village church can be seen ahead. Keep the fence on the left now, head for a stile and continue beside the river. Follow the path down to the water's edge and make for a kissing gate. Cross the Leven by a pretty weir and follow the road through Great Ayton.

20 Roseberry Topping

Roseberry Topping, one of the National Park's most famous landmarks, dominates much of this outstanding walk, which starts off by skirting the towering peak's lower flank, heading for the extensive tree cover of Hutton Lowcross Woods. Bypassing sleepy Hutton Village, the route begins the return leg by climbing through Hutton Wood to the edge of open moorland where it joins the Cleveland Way, bound for Roseberry Topping.

Distance:
5 miles/8km
Height gain:
655ft/200m
Walking time:
2$\frac{1}{2}$-2$\frac{3}{4}$ hours
Start/Finish: Newton under Roseberry car

park. GR571121.
Type of walk: Clear paths and forest bridleways, followed by a section of the Cleveland Way. A paved path zigzags to Roseberry Topping's summit.

Driven by a restless spirit and an unquenchable thirst for adventure, James Cook almost certainly climbed to the lofty vantage point of Roseberry Topping as a boy. Etched into his memory, the views from the top would have served as a nostalgic reminder of home when, in later life, Cook travelled the high seas in search of distant, undiscovered lands. Once quarried for alum, jet and iron ore, Roseberry Topping rises to over 1,000ft/305m. Part of the peak collapsed during mining excavations, resulting in its distinctive, jutting profile.

Make for a track at the northern end of the car park and turn right. Roseberry Topping's summit looms ahead, like a dormant volcano. Follow the track through a gate, avoiding some steps leading up to a National Trust sign in the trees. Stay on the track, skirting the woodland, and strike out along the hill's lower flank. Pass through a gate and continue as the track tapers to a path.

Merge with another path and keep the boundary on the left. The bracken-clad slopes of Roseberry Topping still dominate the view to the right. On reaching a gate, by a National Trust sign, continue ahead on the waymarked path, cutting between Hanging Stone Wood and a drystone wall. Disregard the paths and tracks running off either side and keep ahead, following the bridleway and footpath waymarks. Merge with a forest ride and maintain the same direction. Head straight on when the track loops to the left and this next stage of the walk reveals glimpses of fields between the trees.

The track dwindles to a path, heading for a gate on the edge of the forest. Sweep round to the left and down to the road. Turn right and follow it through a tunnel of trees towards Hutton Village. Pass the village sign and as the road curves left, join a bridleway running up through trees. The rutted track climbs quite steeply; continue ahead at a junction, following the bridleway towards a gate leading on to Hutton Moor.

Do not go through the gate. Instead, turn right and skirt the wood by following a clear track. Continue

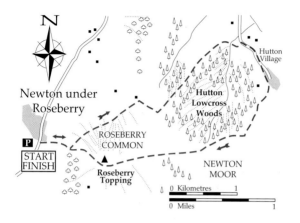

for about 75yds/m, turning left through a gate at the sign for the Cleveland Way. Head out across Newton Moor. This breezy stage of the walk, contrasting markedly with bursts of extensive tree cover, is complemented by some of the finest moorland vistas in the National Park.

Captain Cook's monument can be seen to the left on the far ridge, no more than a slender obelisk at this distance, dwarfed by the hills and the spaciousness of its setting. Roseberry Topping, the walk's final objective, lies ahead.

On reaching a junction of rights of way, avoid the turning on the left for Gribdale and continue on the Cleveland Way towards Roseberry Topping. Follow the paved path to the foot of the hill and begin the climb to the trig pillar on the summit.

From the top of Roseberry Topping, there is a magnificent 360° view of the surrounding countryside.

Even on this lofty hilltop there are ugly reminders of life in the world beyond Roseberry Topping. The rocky platform here is strewn with carved initials and the trig pillar has been daubed with graffiti.

With back to the trig pillar, look for a crumbling paved path on the left, snaking down to the hill foot. Follow this circuitous route, taking care on the descent. Look for a gate by trees at the bottom, continuing on the stepped path as it curves to the right. Avoid a path on the left, running down into the trees, and keep going to the next junction.

Bear left here – there is a path on the right – and head through the woodland. Keep right when the path splits and drop down the bank to a National Trust sign for Roseberry Topping. Pass through the gate and follow the track ahead, returning to the car park at Newton under Roseberry.

21 Kilburn White Horse

From the Kilburn White Horse, this exposed farmland walk heads south-west, crossing the National Park's western boundary to explore an expansive patchwork of fields, trees and hedgerows. The distinctive outline of the White Horse edges into view at intervals before the walk reaches the village of Kilburn, where there is a welcome inn.

Distance: 7 miles/11km
Height gain: 590ft/180m
Walking time: 3 hours
Start/Finish: Kilburn White Horse car park. GR514813.

Type of walk: Below the wooded scarp, the walk follows field paths, bridleways and green lanes to Kilburn village. The last lap follows the initial leg of the walk.

Cut into the limestone escarpment and best appreciated from a distance, the Kilburn White Horse was the brainchild of Thomas Taylor, a local man. The horse, 315ft/96m long and 230ft/70m high, was marked out in 1857 by the local schoolmaster and many of his pupils. In 1925 a restoration fund was subscribed by the readers of the Yorkshire Evening Post, and the residue of £100 was invested to provide for the triennial grooming of the figure. The Vale of York and the distant Pennine chain can be seen from the top.

Leave the car park below the White Horse by joining the road and turning right. Follow it down to a parking sign and bear right where a track crosses the lane. This area is thick with broad-leaved and conifer woodland. Head through trees and keep left when the track forks. Begin a gentle climb, curving gradually to the right, and look for a sign – *dogs must be kept on a lead.*

Turn sharp left here onto a bridleway and follow it down through trees, heading south-east. Keep to the path, cutting along the wooded flank of the escarpment, until a ladder stile comes into view on the right. Unusually, this one is surmounted with a gate. Cross the field to two ladder stiles linked by a bridge, an even more elaborate construction which, from a distance, is oddly reminiscent of something from a children's adventure playground. Its purpose is to deter deer.

Continue ahead and, on drawing level with the farm, veer right to a stile. Cross several enclosures, which can be boggy in places, until the path reaches a pair of gates. Turn right onto a rough track and follow it along the field edge. Make for a gate in the corner, by a derelict animal shelter, and cross a track just beyond it. Strike out along the lower slopes of the valley, heading towards a wood and keeping a ditch on the left. Look for a stile up ahead by trees and cross the little stream. The ground here can be damp and boggy, even in dry conditions.

Continue to maintain the same direction, with the woodland now on the right. Follow a vague path

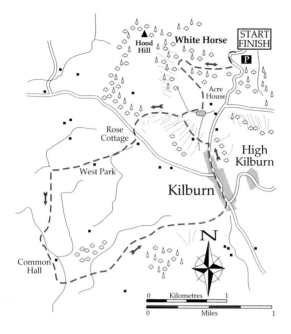

across the rough pasture and look for a stile and gate leading out to the road. Bear left for a few yards, then turn right towards Rose Cottage. Keep to the track as it runs south-west across open farmland. Approach the buildings of West Park, veering right just before them. Skirt the field, keeping the farm on the left, and look for the Pennine chain on the far westerly horizon.

Pass through the gap in the boundary and follow the clear track, initially with a hedgerow on the right. Continue when the unfenced bridleway heads out across open fields. Turn left at the

Kilburn

junction and follow the track towards Kilburn Park. Bear left at the next waymark, passing under some power lines before reaching the buildings of Common Hall. Keep right at the junction and walk along the lane until a bridleway sign is seen on the left. Follow the dirt track as it skirts the field, the figure of the White Horse at Kilburn edging into view on Roulston Scar.

Continue ahead on the track as it crosses and skirts several fields and enclosures. Avoid a track running off to the left by a sturdy oak tree and follow the woodland path until it rejoins the track. Head for the outskirts of Kilburn and turn left at the road. The village is where Robert Thompson, the famous woodcarver, was born in 1876. His renowned trademark signature was in the form of a mouse – the expression "as poor as a church mouse" apparently giving him the inspiration.

Pass the *Foresters Arms Hotel* and the Mouseman Visitor Centre and continue through the village. Cross the North York Moors National Park boundary and take the next signposted track on the left. Follow the track to the double gates on the right, take the path across the fields, head north to the foot of the wooded scarp and retrace the outward leg of the walk back to the car park.

22 Kepwick and the Hambleton Drove Road

This exhilarating walk captures the spirit and character of the Hambleton Hills, illustrating the striking contrast between the limestone escarpment of the high moorland and the vast patchwork plain below. From Kepwick, the route climbs steadily to the Hambleton Drove Road, following it north along the rim of the hills and then west over Kepwick Moor. The final leg crosses open pasture, with fine views across the Vale of York.

Distance:	begins with a gradual
6 miles/9.5km	ascent to the higher
Height gain:	ground of the
655ft/198m	Hambleton Hills.
Walking time:	Heading north, the route
2³/₄-3 hours	follows clear paths,
Start/Finish: Kepwick	tracks and drives before
car park. GR467908.	descending to open
Type of walk: The walk	farmland.

Leave the car park by turning right onto the road, pass the church and continue to a bridleway on the left. Go through the white gate and follow the route up between gorse bushes to a second gate. Keep going on the sunken path, cutting through rhododendron bushes and over open moorland to run between woodland and a drystone wall. Pass a waymarked path on the right and continue on the bridleway, following it alongside Cowesby Wood.

Make for another gate and keep going through the bracken, climbing gradually and curving to the left. The outline of Kepwick Hall can be glimpsed down to the left, amid trees. Pass a footpath and gate on the left and continue ahead, merging with a track. Keep right when it forks and head through the trees. Avoid a cycle trail shooting off to the left and continue for about 100yds/m to a junction with the Cleveland Way. Turn left and follow the Hambleton Drove Road, a broad grassy track on this stretch.

The precise age of the Hambleton Drove Road is not known but it was certainly in use during the Bronze Age and the Roman Occupation. It also played a key role in the transportation of sheep and cattle, with 18th and 19th century drovers opting for this route to avoid costly turnpike tolls on their way from Scotland to the sheep fairs at York and Malton and the cattle markets further south. In spring the foot of the scarp is carpeted with cowslips, primroses and violets – among other colourful flowers.

Pass a bridleway on the left and keep going in a northerly direction. A white gate and sign for Kepwick come into view further on. The track on the right is signposted *Hawnby*. Continue on the Cleveland Way until two gates are seen on the left. Leave the long-distance path at the second one and follow the grassy track alongside the wall, with a superb view of Kepwick Moor adding an extra dimension to the spectacular surroundings.

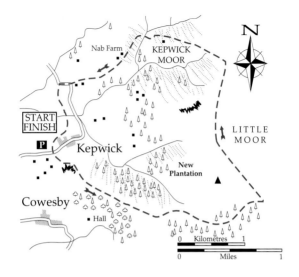

Keep going alongside the plantation and the buildings of Nab Farm can be seen down below in the distance. Pass a sign *beware adders* at the next gate and drop down to a cinder track, following it over a gill and round to the farm. Keep to the left of the outbuildings and join the main drive. Bear right by Cross Lodge and follow the road to the next right-hand bend. Go through the white gate and turn immediately left, crossing the field to a stile beneath the branches of an oak tree.

Head diagonally across the next field to a footbridge in the tree-lined boundary. Cross the Bridge Beck, aim slightly left to the next stile and then veer obliquely right in the next field. Look for a stile beneath some power lines and head diagonally left up the hillside. Make for a stile midway between some farm outbuildings and a clump of trees. There is a delightful view of Kepwick's surrounding countryside from the hill crest. Veer over to the left boundary, where a waymark is visible among the trees. Turn left at the stile and return to the car park along the street.

23 Clay Bank Top and Urra Moor

This bracing walk is enhanced by some of the finest and most dramatic upland scenery in the National Park. From Clay Bank Top, the route heads for gentle farmland before climbing up to Round Hill, the highest point on the North York Moors. The home stretch begins by crossing Urra Moor to the tiny settlement of Urra, sheltering in the shadow of Hasty Bank.

Distance:
9½ miles/15km
Height gain:
655ft/198m
Walking time:
5-5½ hours
Start/Finish: Clay Bank
Top car park. GR572036.

Type of walk: A moderate walk, consisting of sheltered paths, the trackbed of a disused railway and a very open, exposed stretch of the Cleveland Way.

Clay Bank Top offers breathtaking views over this corner of the North York Moors. The Cleveland Plain stretches to the far horizon, with Roseberry Topping's prominent peak reaching skyward.

Leave the car park and take the road on the immediate left – signposted *alternative car park*. Follow the lane down through the woods, with the scarp of the Cleveland Hills rising against the skyline. Pass the car park and continue along to West Wood Farm.

Turn right, following the drive through the farmyard and then along an avenue of poplar trees. Passing a duck pond, the path cuts across several pastures to emerge on a lane, opposite the turning to Woods Farm. Bear right, follow the road for about 200yds/m, then turn left at the footpath sign and keep the field boundary on the left. Cross the Ingleby Beck via a footbridge and continue ahead over several more pastures to reach the cinder trackbed of the former Ironstone Railway.

The railway, used to transport ironstone from the Rosedale mines to blast furnaces in the industrial North-East, was finally taken out of service in the late 1920s. Looking at the dramatic 700ft escarpment, it is hard to believe that loaded railway wagons were lowered down here at an angle of 1 in 5.

Bear right, keep left at the fork and follow the old line up to Incline Top, continuing to a junction with the Cleveland Way. Turn sharp right and follow the path in a westerly direction. Keep right at the fork and head over Round Hill, the trig pillar and cairn here indicating a height of 1,490ft/454m. Continue on the Cleveland Way towards the shoulder of Hasty Bank, with its alum spoil heaps dating back to the 17th century. To the right the Cleveland Plain stretches to the horizon, a glorious patchwork of fields, trees and hedgerows.

On reaching a bridleway finger post, 30yds/m before a gate, turn sharp left and follow the path

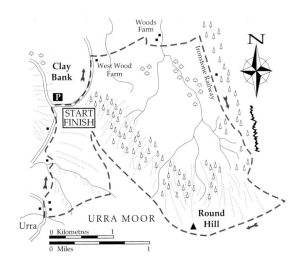

along the edge of Urra Moor, keeping a ditch on the right. Descend through the heather, at one point curving a little to the right; ahead is the outline of a moorland ravine, the walk's next objective. Cross it and continue on the path, keeping the beck on the right.

The buildings of Urra edge into sight, no more than a tiny hamlet at the foot of Hasty Bank. Look for a bridleway sign ahead, turn right and follow the sunken path down towards Urra. Follow the path as it curves left, leading down to a gate on the right, just before a plantation.

Take the grassy path and aim for a gate by Urra House. Turn right at the lane and follow it round the left bend. Two footpaths can be seen on the right, denoted by waymarks. Keep right, crossing a stile, and continue on the well-defined path into a pretty wood. Cross a scurrying beck by the footbridge and negotiate the next stile on the right.

Follow the path between woodland and wall, heading down to a gate leading on to a track. Turn right and walk along the waymarked track to the road where it meets the Cleveland Way. Bear right and return to the car park.

24 Osmotherley

Cod Beck Reservoir's superb moorland setting is the first of many treats offered by this splendid walk. The path follows the water's edge before crossing open farmland to join the well-trodden Cleveland Way. From here there are stunning views across the Vale of York. After a short detour to a secret chapel, and a visit to the village of Osmotherley, the route springs one final surprise – a glorious woodland walk back to the reservoir.

Distance: 4 miles/6.5km **Height gain:** 251ft/77m **Walking time:** 2¼ hours **Start/Finish:** Cod Beck Reservoir, near Osmotherley. GR466993. Start at northern end of lake.	**Type of walk:** The walk skirts Cod Beck Reservoir before following field paths to the route of the Cleveland Way. Beyond Osmotherley, paths lead up to the edge of open moorland.

Follow the permitted path alongside the lake to its southern end, keeping the road close by on the right. Pass the dam and look for a kissing gate leading out to the road.

Bear sharp right to the footpath sign; turn left here and head up the rough pasture, following the wall round to the right. The path can be seen ahead, cutting through gorse and light woodland.

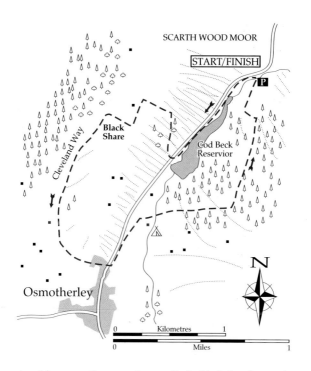

Avoid a path running off half left through undergrowth and with the wall just below on the right and the reservoir still visible, begin to curve left, heading up the gentle rise towards a bracken-covered pit on the edge of a disused quarry.

Swing right to a stile and waymark, skirting the field to a gate. There is a splendid view from here down towards Cod Beck Reservoir, with thickly afforested slopes rising above it. On the far horizon is the jutting peak of Roseberry Topping.

Bear left along the lane, heading south, and continue as far as two adjoining gates on the right. Take the furthest wooden gate and skirt the field, with a BT transmitter station visible on the right. Make for a gate in the corner and join a path cutting between carpets of bracken.

Turn left on reaching the Cleveland Way and follow it down through coniferous woodland, emerging at a kissing gate. There is a magnificent view to the west here, across the busy A19 to a distant patchwork of field patterns. Go through the gate and keep the view to the right. Keep left on reaching some farm outbuildings and continue on the Cleveland Way. Bear sharp left at the sign for the Lady Chapel and follow the stony track.

Stanley Bond

Osmotherley

Rebuilt during the 1950s and rededicated in 1961, the Lady Chapel has been a place of pilgrimage for 600 years. Carthusian monks were drawn to this peaceful, undisturbed setting when they founded the nearby Mount Grace Priory in the 14th century. The door to the Lady Chapel is always open to those seeking the opportunity for quiet prayer and reflection.

The Yorkshire Dales, York Minster and Durham Cathedral can be seen from this spot on a good day. Take the track back to the route of the Cleveland Way and continue towards Osmotherley. Turn right at the junction to visit the village centre, characterised by its market cross and stone table, once used to display produce, then walk back along the road, passing endless rows of pretty stone cottages before the speed de-restriction sign is reached. Follow the pavement as far as the right-hand turning for Cote Ghyll Caravan Park and Osmotherley Youth Hostel.

Follow the uneven track alongside the entrance to the caravan site and keep to the left of the youth hostel building. Veer up the bank on a footpath as the track approaches a white gate leading to a private house. Follow the path through trees and ahead is a gate, with a sign for Cod Beck Reservoir. Pass alongside the crumbling remains of a stone wall, covered with lichen, and continue on the path as it curves right through a bracken glade. On reaching the next main junction, by the shell of a stone byre, turn left and follow the track to another sign for the reservoir.

Disregard the permitted path on the left and

continue ahead on the right of way. Go straight on when the track bends right and begin to drop down the slope. There are glimpses of Scarth Wood Moor between the trees. Swing left about 30yds/m before a ladder-stile and take the path through the plantation, towards a visible picnic table and bench by the edge of the reservoir. Look for an obvious path on the right and follow it down through trees to a kissing gate. Cross the beck just beyond it and return to the parking area.

25 Carlton Bank

A superb, high-level walk encapsulating all the rugged beauty and majestic scenery of the North York Moors. Starting at Carlton Bank, the route follows the dramatic scarp of the Cleveland Hills for several miles before descending to the villages of Faceby, Carlton-in-Cleveland and Kirkby. The walk finishes with a dramatic climb to Cringle Moor. This is true adventure country – an obvious draw for those who love the high tops and desolate places of Britain's upland regions.

Distance:	Bank. GR522033.
11 miles/18km	***Type of walk:*** *A stretch*
Height gain:	*of the Cleveland Way*
452ft/138m	*along the rim of the*
Walking time:	*Cleveland Hills*
6-6½ hours	*escarpment, field paths,*
Start/Finish: *Lord*	*tracks and a section of*
Stones car park, Carlton	*paved causeway.*

From Lord Stones car park, cross the road and join the route of the Cleveland Way. Begin the first climb, making for the trig pillar on the summit of Carlton Bank, one of the National Park's most popular landmarks. This stretch of the escarpment, criss-crossed by jet miners' tracks and littered with the spoils of alum mining, provides a fascinating insight into the area's industrial past. Over to the left are the headquarters of the Teesside and Newcastle Gliding Club. Keep going, following the path down Faceby Bank and over the slopes of

Gold Hill. Veer right at the fork, keeping alongside a forest boundary fence.

Look for a waymarked wicket gate and drop down dramatically through the trees of Faceby Plantation to reach Bank Lane. Pass the buildings of High Farm and continue along the lane to Faceby. Follow the road through the village, avoid Mill Lane and head north-west towards the A172. Take the first waymarked path on the right and follow it for 1 mile/1.6km, crossing several field enclosures to reach the pretty village of Carlton-in-Cleveland.

Sheltering in the lee of the Cleveland Hills, Carlton-in-Cleveland is a mecca for keen walkers and visitors. The unusually-named Blackwell Ox pub in the main street takes its name from a weighty shorthorn bull bred in the Darlington area. Once an important centre for alum mining, the village boasts a notable late 19th century Gothic church.

Leave Carlton by following the path alongside the Methodist chapel. Once clear of the village, the walk enters a gentle world of endless field pastures, dominated by teasing glimpses of Roseberry Topping on the horizon. On reaching Kirkby, turn right in the village centre and follow the paved causeway towards the vast bulk of Cringle Moor. This ancient trade route was regularly used by travellers and panniermen as they made their way across the moors, to and from the coast.

Pass Manor Farm and Kirby Grange and continue to the caravan park at Toft Hill. Follow the path

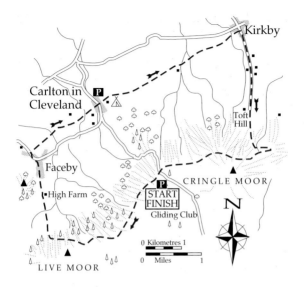

alongside the wall and then up the stone-stepped path to reach the Cleveland Way at the point where it crosses 1,400ft Cringle Moor. The remains of alum craters can be seen carved into the landscape. Follow the long-distance path in a westerly direction, the scenery on this stretch of the route never less than magnificent. The walk's next objective is Cringle End, a favourite vantage point with walkers on the Cleveland Way. The stone seat here commemorates Alec Falconer, a local resident, and founder member of the Middlesbrough Rambling Club, who died in 1968. From here the Cleveland Way descends to the road and Lord Stones car park.

Useful Information

Youth Hostels

Osmotherley: Cote Ghyll, Osmotherley, Northallerton, DL6 3AH (01609) 883575

Helmsley: Carlton Lane, Helmsley, YO6 5HB (01439) 770433

Wheeldale: Wheeldale Lodge, Goathland, Whitby, YO22 5AP (01947) 896350

Lockton: The Old School, Lockton, Pickering, YO18 7PY (01751) 460376

Scarborough: The White House, Burniston Road, Scarborough, YO13 ODA (01723) 361176

Boggle Hole: Boggle Hole, Mill Beck, Fylingthorpe, Whitby, YO22 4UQ (01947) 880352

Whitby: East Cliff, Whitby, YO22 4JT (01947) 602878

Camping Barns

Farndale: (01751) 433053

Kildale: (01642) 722135

Northallerton: (01609) 772311

Sinnington: (01751) 473792

Westerdale: (01287) 660259

Tourist Information Centres

Great Ayton: High Green Car Park (01642) 722835

Guisborough: Priory Grounds, Church St (01287) 633801

Helmsley: Market Place (01439) 770173

Pickering: Eastgate Car Park (01751) 473791

Scarborough: Pavilion House, Valley Bridge Road (01723) 373333

Sutton Bank: (01845) 597426

Thirsk: Kirkgate (01845) 522755

Whitby: Langborne Road (01947) 602674

Other Visitor and Information Centres

Danby: The North York Moors Centre (01287) 660654

Goathland: Moors Outdoor Centre (01947) 896459

Hutton-le-Hole: Ryedale Folk Museum (01751) 417367

Low Dalby: Dalby Forest Visitor Centre (01751) 460295

Ravenscar: The National Trust Coastal Centre (01723) 870138

Public Transport

The Moorsbus is operated by the North York Moors National Park Authority, The Old Vicarage, Bondgate, Helmsley, York YO6 5BP

(01439) 770657, or contact a National Park Visitor Centre.

To avoid disappointment, parties of 6 or more are asked to telephone the National Park Authority before planning their trip.

For information about the North York Moors Railway, telephone (01751) 472508

For times of trains in the region, call the National Train Information line on 0345 48 49 50.

Weather

It is advisable to call the weather forecast on 0891 500418 before setting off on a walk.

Miscellaneous

Tom Leonard Mining Museum: Skinningrove
(01287) 642877

Captain Cook Schoolroom Museum: Great Ayton
(01642) 722030

Acknowledgements

I would like to express my gratitude to all those people who gave their time and demonstrated their expertise during the preparation of this book – in particular Geri Coop of the North York Moors National Park Authority, Brian Walker of Forest Enterprise and Angie Boast of North York Moors Railway Enterprises. I would also like to thank Robin and Marjorie Prout of Kirkbymoorside for their kindness, Mulgrave Estates for granting permission to use the railway track at Runswick Bay, and Scarborough Borough Council for giving permission to include the disused railway track between Scarborough and Whitby.

This book is dedicated to all those people I met and befriended while staying in the region's youth hostels.